Children with Emotional and
Behavioural Difficulties

Children with Emotional and Behavioural Difficulties:
Strategies for Assessment and Intervention

Edited By

Peter Farrell

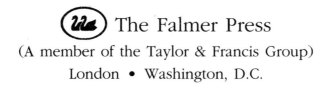

The Falmer Press

(A member of the Taylor & Francis Group)

London • Washington, D.C.

UK   The Falmer Press, 4 John Street, London WC1N 2ET
USA   The Falmer Press, Taylor & Francis Inc., 1900 Frost Road, Suite 101,
      Bristol, PA 19007

First published in 1995

**A catalogue record for this book is available from the British
Library**

**Library of Congress Cataloging-in-Publication Data are
available on request**

ISBN 0 7507 0361 x cased
ISBN 0 7507 0362 8 paper

Jacket design by Caroline Archer

Typeset in 10/12 pt Garamond by
Graphicraft Typesetters Ltd., Hong Kong.

*Printed in Great Britain by Burgess Science Press, Basingstoke on
paper which has a specified pH value on final paper manufacture
of not less than 7.5 and is therefore 'acid free'.*

Contents

Contents

Preface

Children with emotional and behavioural difficulties (EBD) pose a continuing challenge to their parents, teachers, support services and LEAs. As will be seen later in this book there is evidence that the numbers of children being referred for some form of special help are increasing, that their problems are more intractable and that children appear to be displaying problems at a younger age. More and more children are now being excluded from school and there is national concern about the truancy figures.

Various reasons have been put forward to explain this trend and these are explored later in this book. It is possible that increases in the number of children labelled as being EBD may be associated with a general increase in disaffection felt by many people across the whole country which is associated with high levels of unemployment, increasing homelessness and an ever rising crime rate. Against these societal pressures it is not always easy for teachers, schools and LEAs to find solutions to problems facing them. However, this book seeks to address these issues by focusing on ways in which children with EBD can be helped within the current climate.

Indeed the government has been active in finding ways to help schools and LEAs address these problems. The Code of Practice on the identification and assessment of children with special needs and the Circulars on pupils with problems directly focus on issues such as the definition of EBD, on ways in which schools can develop discipline policies, on how schools can provide effective strategies to help children whose behaviour is troublesome and on exclusions. The government has also provided extra resources to LEAs to help them address the truancy problem. The potential impact of recent government initiatives is referred to throughout the book.

The book as a whole is divided into three sections. Chapters 1–4 focus mainly on assessment issues, chapters 5–8 on aspects of intervention and chapters 9–12 on how schools and LEAs as a whole can effect the lives of children with emotional and behaviour problems. There is, however, some overlap between the sections which reflects the fact that the whole subject is complex and is not easily divided into neat compartments.

The reader will detect some common themes which permeate the whole book and reflect its overall ethos. The first of these is the belief that government legislation, in particular the 1988 Education Act, may have contributed to the rise in problem behaviour in schools. The climate created by a market led education system does not favour the vulnerable and disadvantaged, in particular pupils with EBD. There is therefore a belief that the government, by its actions in legislating for change in education, has made the situation worse for these children, their teachers and their parents.

The second permeating theme of the book is the recognition that children with EBD come from socially and economically disadvantaged families whose parents are not usually well educated and who may themselves have experienced problems in school. Such parents are not likely to lobby for better services for their children and form pressure groups. Instead they may be viewed as outsiders, who do not cooperate with the system and who therefore form a convenient scapegoat and focus for blame for the behaviour of their children.

The third theme concerns the problems that all professionals face in coming to an acceptable definition of emotional and behaviour problems. This has implications for assessment, and conflicts about definition can lead to professionals having different opinions as to how such children should be helped.

The fourth theme is a concern that pupils with EBD may not have an equal opportunity to assessment and provision. The number of boys being referred for help greatly outnumbers girls and there is a real concern that the needs of girls with emotional problems are not being addressed, perhaps because their problems do not often cause problems for their teachers. Similarly, there is concern that pupils from black and other ethnic minority communities are not dealt with in the same way as their white counterparts.

The final theme that runs through the whole book is both optimistic and challenging. This is the belief that schools and LEAs can make a substantial contribution in the prevention of emotional and behaviour difficulties. This is optimistic because it is saying that schools can and should make a difference. However, it is a challenge as schools have to find ways of addressing the issues, of considering how their existing practices might change and to resist blaming others, for example the government, the families or society for the problems which they face.

This book is not, and never was, intended to answer all the problems faced by parents, teachers, support services and LEAs who work with EBD children. Instead the aim has been to highlight current issues that are of concern to all professionals who work in this area and to offer some further insights as to how the education for these children can be improved.

Chapter 1

Emotional and Behavioural Difficulties: Causes, Definition and Assessment

Peter Farrell

Introduction

As stated in the preface to this volume, pupils with emotional and behavioural problems continue to pose a challenge for teachers, support services, the community and for their parents. There is evidence that the number of pupils being referred to educational psychologists is increasing, McCall and Farrell (1993) and that more are being excluded from schools, Upton (1992). Scarcely a week goes by without sections of the media reporting on incidents of disruption in schools and these reports are usually accompanied by suggestions about various ways of improving the situation. These range from exhortations to bring back corporal punishment, to ban children from obtaining copies of so called video nasties, to reduce the amount of violence shown on television, to sack incompetent teachers, to improve the quality of training and many others. Interest in this area is also evidenced by the number of training packages for teachers which are designed to improve their skills in managing disruptive children. Many of these are based on principles of behavioural psychology, for example BATPACK (Wheldall and Merrett, 1989a and 1989b); *Assertive Discipline* (Canter and Canter, 1992). Others emphasize a whole school approach, for example, *Preventative Approaches to Disruption*, (Chisholm *et al.*, 1985), *Building a Better Behaved School*, (Galvin *et al.*, 1990). Finally the government has issued six circulars on pupils with problems which offer guidance to schools and LEAs on the education of children with EBD (DFE, 1994).

It has been argued by McCall and Farrell (1993) and Upton (1992) that one major consequence of the 1988 Education Act has been an increase in the referral of children with EBD for special educational provision. This legislation has introduced a 'market led' philosophy in which schools compete with each other for children, where exam results are published and where 'excellence' in education is measured solely in terms of academic criteria. In this climate it is hardly surprising that schools are tempted to direct their resources towards meeting the needs of their more able pupils with less help being offered to the more vulnerable particularly to pupils whose behaviour is likely to disrupt the smooth running of a school. Hence these children are referred to support services, in particular educational psychologists, in the hope and expectation that they will be removed to a special school or unit. It is unlikely that mainstream schools will resist this trend by aiming to become centres of excellence in the education and treatment of unruly and disturbed children. However laudable that aim, it will not impress prospective parents who, on the whole, would prefer their children to be educated alongside a well behaved, motivated and highly achieving peer group.

This last point leads us on to one of the key issues facing parents and professionals who work with children with EBD. If we contrast the public's response to this group when compared with, for example, children with physical difficulties or Down's syndrome, we often find for these latter groups that there is a feeling that we as a society have a responsibility to care and to help. Consequently if a mainstream school prides itself in offering support, for example, to children with physical difficulties, its reputation is unlikely to be damaged and may even be enhanced. The same could not be said for pupils with EBD or even perhaps for children with moderate learning difficulties. If the 'blame' for the disorder does not lie with the child or family and may be genetic or due to a birth injury or a road traffic accident, then we all feel we should help as no one is responsible for causing the problem. However with EBD the 'blame' is often levelled at someone, frequently the parents or the child, and teachers may be less inclined to offer help and sympathy.

It is also the case, as will be discussed later in this chapter, that pupils with EBD tend to come from economically and socially disadvantaged families. Typically their parents may themselves have disliked school and feel uneasy in the company of other more educated professionals such as teachers and psychologists. These parents may find it difficult to articulate their hopes and fears for their children and to form pressure groups for better services. This is in marked contrast to families of children with, for example, dyslexia or autism. Without the support of similar pressure groups there is a danger that services for children with EBD will suffer, that they will be denied access to integrated education and that resources will be directed elsewhere.

It is against this background of increasing concern about children with emotional and behavioural problems that it is important to discuss some of the key issues which underpin our work with this group. Firstly, what are the causes of EBD; secondly, is it possible to arrive at an accepted definition of the term and thirdly how can we assess the extent of the problem and how does our assessment inform intervention? The Code of Practice for identifying SEN came into force in September 1994 and a new circular on EBD has just been issued. These provide a useful starting point for considering these issues in greater depth. In this chapter I shall briefly review the causes of EBD before moving on to a more lengthy discussion on definition and assessment.

Causes of Emotional and Behavioural Difficulties

When discussing the causes of emotional and behavioural difficulties it is important to recognize that there are likely to be a number of interrelated factors to consider. Indeed, Cooper (1993) suggests that problem behaviours are a result of a complex 'interaction between contextual factors and aspects which the individual brings to the situation' (p. 9). In particular the home environment and the school can play a large part in shaping the social and emotional adjustment of children. These two factors interact with the child's own genetic predisposition.

Home Environment

As mentioned in the introduction to this chapter, it is well known that children in EBD schools tend to come from socially and economically disadvantaged families. Cooper (1993) has summarized some of the evidence which shows that such children are likely to have experienced:

- lack of parental interest in schooling;
- inconsistent and ineffectual parental discipline;
- lack of overtly displayed parental affection;
- parental indifference, hostility or rejection;
- violent displays of temper from the parents;
- parental use of corporal punishment;
- parental cruelty or neglect;
- parental absences;
- rejecting and violent parents.

(See Reid, 1987; Herbert, 1993; and many others for a more thorough review of research evidence.)

It is tempting when reading through the above list to place all the blame on parents for their children's problems. However these parents may themselves have experienced problems in childhood and as adults they may have problems in coping with day-to-day life to the extent that there is little space left to devote to being an effective and loving parent. Their child's school problems may be insignificant when set against the mountain of other more pressing concerns. In this environment children can model themselves on the culture of their community accepting and embracing its norms and patterns of behaviour which may be contradictory to the academically orientated and conformist value system of the school. In this atmosphere parents' apparent unwillingness to cooperate with schools should not be seen as a sign of indifference and it is important for teachers and other agencies to try to work with and support families so as to help them overcome any feelings of indifference or even hostility that they may have.

School Factors

There is now a great deal of evidence to suggest that schools can play a vital role in causing and therefore preventing EBD. Early work by Reynolds and Sullivan (1981) and Rutter *et al.* (1979) shows that schools from similar catchment areas experience different rates of truancy, and behaviour problems. This was confirmed by a recent HMI report entitled *Education for Disaffected Pupils* (DFE, 1993) which focused on pupils' behaviour in thirty-one primary and eighteen secondary schools. In this survey satisfactory standards of behaviour were associated with the following features:

- most teachers enjoyed the company of other pupils and were interested in them;
- classrooms were orderly places;
- pupils were punctual and attended regularly;
- a wide range of formal and informal rewards were used and applied consistently by the majority of staff;
- sanctions were fair, understood by pupils and parents, proportionate to the offence and were applied flexibly and constructively;
- the curriculum was generally matched to the pupils' needs, abilities and aptitudes;
- lessons were well prepared and clearly delivered through an appropriate range of teaching styles;
- teachers were secure in the knowledge of their subject;
- the marking of pupils' work was constructive with regular feedback being given on both the quality of its presentation and on the attainment;
- standards of achievement were either satisfactory or better;
- there was a programme of extra curricular activities which was effective in building up the confidence of pupils, their self esteem and in promoting cooperative relationships.

Unsatisfactory standards of behaviour were associated with the following:

- lessons had staggered beginnings because of late arrivals and unauthorized departures;
- few staff had the skills to defuse potentially difficult situations and on occasion fuelled them by an inappropriate confrontational stance;
- some teachers made threats which they couldn't carry out;
- many pupils were critical of the capacity of staff to control them;
- standards of achievement were unsatisfactory;
- pupils and staff attendance were poor and morale was at a low ebb.

How schools reach the positions outlined above is a complex question. As discussed earlier in this chapter, there can be no doubt that the home background plays a part in establishing the attitude and motivation towards school of many pupils. If the pupils' attitude to school is indifferent or even negative, this clearly makes the teachers' task more difficult and without a great deal of support and further training, they may become demoralized and feel under-valued. This can lead to them putting less into the job than they might do in different circumstances and as a result their schools display the factors iden-tified by HMI in the ones whose behaviour was less satisfactory. As a result a vicious circle can become established with the best teachers being promoted to schools in 'better' areas and those who remain struggle to cope as well as they can being additionally disadvantaged in the competitive climate engen-dered by the 1988 Education Act. In this way it is easy to see how the 'good' schools can get better and the 'bad' schools become worse. Fortunately this gloomy scenario is countered to some extent by the findings of the studies by Reynolds and Sullivan (1981) and Rutter *et al.* (1979) which clearly indicate that even with schools in extremely poor catchment areas the attainment and behaviour of the pupils can vary considerably. Schools therefore make a difference and the factors highlighted by the HMI survey give clear guidance on the steps they can take to improve the behaviour of their pupils.

Within Child Factors

Although the home environment and the school can play a large part in causing EBD, we have all met children who come from families where the parents are supportive and where the school is well thought of, who nevertheless display serious emotional and behavioural difficulties. In these cases there may be a significant inherited or constitutional explanation for their problems. Indeed within child causes of EBD tend to be associated with the most serious forms of emotional disturbance. Such children may be labelled as being 'mentally ill' and receive treatment in psychiatric hospitals; they tend to form only a tiny minority of children with emotional and behavioural difficulties.

However, even when the cause is largely 'within child' there are likely to be other factors in the home and the school which have influenced the nature of the problem. Indeed, as suggested throughout this brief review of the causes of EBD, it is virtually impossible to attribute them to one factor alone as there is almost always a large interaction between them. It is also important to remember that our own perceptions of what might cause EBD can influence the development of a pupil's behaviour. If we expect children from 'poor' areas to have behaviour problems then, quite unknowingly, we may interact with them in a way which will validate our predictions. This is sometimes referred to as a self-fulfilling prophecy. As professionals we should always be aware of the potential effects of our beliefs and prejudices on the behaviour of children.

It can be seen that the issue of what causes EBD is by no means a simple question and that in order to understand a child who has problems we need to keep an open mind, be aware of our prejudices and how they can effect our judgment and be sensitive to the way in which the various factors within the child's the home background and the school may influence his or her behaviour.

Defining Emotional and Behavioural Difficulties

The term emotional and behavioural difficulties is similar to all types of SEN in that there is no hard and fast cut-off point between a child who is or is not perceived as EBD. This continuum of need is enshrined in government legislation and by the guidance emanating from the 1993 Act. The Circular on EBD (DFE, 1994) reinforces the point about EBD being on a continuum but even so it suggests that there are three 'types' of EBD.

The first could be described as problems that are a response to recent stresses and strains in a child's life, for example the death of a parent or a recent change of school. Such problems are usually short lived and with sensitive and careful handling they should be overcome. All of us have encountered problems in our lives that have caused us to behave in ways we may subsequently regret and which could be described by others as being indicative of some emotional disturbance. However we would be unlikely to be described as having emotional and behaviour problems.

The second group of children are likely to have long standing problems which are more deep seated. They may require a more detailed assessment of their needs and other agencies may become involved. Such children may be referred for statutory assessment. The third group, which make up a tiny minority of cases, are more seriously disturbed and may have some psychiatric problems, for example anorexia or childhood schizophrenia. Teachers are most likely to encounter children in the first two groups.

However, definitions of EBD also depend to a great extent on our perception of what is normal and acceptable behaviour. There is no objective and measurable reality about EBD. Our views about what is normal and acceptable are influenced by our experiences as children, parents, members of society and professionals. For example many people think it is normal and acceptable for a parent to slap his/her child others may disagree and label the behaviour as abusive. Some teachers will think the level of noise in a class is too high, others may not. Some parents may not think it is a problem if their child does not complete homework, teachers will have a different view. Some pupils may think it is alright to leave the class without asking for permission, teachers may not agree. How a school defines problem behaviours depends on the rules and standards of behaviour which it establishes. These are often discussed among staff but seldom with pupils and parents. If children fail to conform to these rules they may be labelled as a problem, even as EBD. However it may not be that the child has a problem but that the rules themselves are unfair and that in another school with different rules the same child would not be labelled as a problem. Furthermore the accepted rules and standards of behaviour at home may be very different from those of the school. Therefore there is no easily agreed and 'objective' definition of EBD as the term is essentially a product of the interaction between the child's family and school and their individual or collective views of normality.

Having considered some general issues to do with the definition of EBD, we shall now look in a little more depth into the definition referred to in the Code of Practice on the Identification and Assessment of Special Educational Needs (DFE, 1994) and in the Circular on EBD (DFE, 1994). The definition of SEN enshrined in the 1993 Education Act remains the same as it is in previous legislation. This definition is presented in full below.

A child has SEN if he or she has a learning difficulty which calls for special educational provision to be made for him or her.

A child has a learning difficulty if he or she:

(a) has a significantly greater difficulty in learning than the majority of children of the same age;

(b) has a disability which either prevents or hinders the child from making use of educational facilities of a kind provided for children of the same age in schools within the area of the local authority;

(c) is under 5 and falls within the definition at (a) or (b) above or would do so if special provision was not made for the child.

A child must not be regarded as having a learning difficulty solely because the language or form of language of the home is different from the language in which he or she will be taught.

Special educational provision means:

(a) for a child over two, educational provision which is additional to, or otherwise different from, the educational provision made generally for children of the child's age in maintained schools, other than special schools in the area;

(b) for a child under two educational provision of any kind.

This definition firmly establishes that all pupils with SEN must have a learning difficulty. This restriction poses something of a problem when defining children with EBD. It is certainly true that the majority of children defined as EBD do indeed experience learning problems but there are also children of above average attainments and ability who experience emotional and adjustment difficulties. To say that these children don't have EBD may result in them being denied access to facilities and resources. To look for evidence of a discrepancy between a child's ability and attainment as part of the evidence for defining a child as having EBD may be inappropriate. The problem lies in the definition

Peter Farrell

of the term 'learning difficulty'. If this is taken to mean a difficulty in learning academic subjects and is tied into an assessment of cognitive ability, then the above concerns would apply. However if the term is widened to include difficulties in *learning* to adjust to the social context in which the child lives and works; problems in *learning* to make and keep friends or in *learning* to follow the normal and accepted patterns of behaviour in a school or family, then it is easier to accept the term 'learning difficulty' as central to the definition of EBD. The Code of Practice and subsequent government publications should make this point clear. Currently the concept of EBD sits uneasily within the legal definition of SEN.

So far we have discussed some of the general issues to do with the definition of EBD. The Code of Practice and the Circular on EBD provide more detailed guidelines as to the specific criteria for proceeding to statutory assessment for all children with SEN including those with EBD. These guidelines therefore give an indication of the extent of EBD problems which might lead to a child receiving a statement. Clearly these children's problems will have persisted over time and schools should have implemented stages 1 to 3 of the assessment procedures outlined in the Code of Practice.

In order to proceed to a statutory assessment for children who may have EBD LEAs are urged by the Code to seek to establish, for example, whether:

- there is a significant discrepancy between the child's cognitive ability (and expectations of the child) and his or her academic attainment;
- the child is unusually withdrawn, lacks confidence or is unable to form purposeful and lasting relationships with peers and adults;
- there is evidence of severely impaired social interaction or communication or a significantly restricted repertoire of activities, interests and imaginative development;
- the child attends school irregularly: the LEA will wish to establish whether there is any pattern to or cause of the child's non-attendance;
- there is recorded evidence of obsessional eating habits;
- there is substance misuse;
- the child displays unpredictable, bizarre, obsessive, violent or severely disruptive behaviour;
- the child has participated in or been subjected to bullying at school; has been subject to neglect and/or abuse at home; and/or has faced major difficulties at home such as parental illness;
- there is evidence that the child may have a significant mental health problem.

In addition, the LEA will need to establish whether and how the school has tried to help the child so far; in particular whether specific programmes have been tried and monitored, whether the parents and pupils have been fully consulted and whether and to what extent outside agencies have been involved.

This guidance is not intended to be exhaustive but should guide schools and other agencies who are planning to proceed to a statutory assessment. The inappropriateness of suggesting a cognitive assessment in the guidelines has been discussed earlier in this chapter.

Among the other guidelines in the list perhaps the most important are those which refer to the child's problems in making relationships and those which refer to his/her response to intervention programmes which have already been implemented. Indeed children with EBD have fundamental problems in forming and sustaining meaningful and mutually rewarding relationships. They may display acting out aggressive and disruptive behaviours or they may be excessively withdrawn. These behaviours have generally persisted for some time despite, or sometimes because of, the efforts of others to help.

Figures on children who are referred for statutory assessment (see Houghton *et al.*, *1988*) show that boys outnumber girls by about six to one and that the majority display acting out behaviour problems. The implications for assessment and intervention of the large difference in the number of girls and boys labelled EBD is discussed at length by Malcolm and Haddock (1992). Children may be referred when their 'problems' are of the acting out variety as these cause difficulties for schools who see the referral as leading to the child being removed. Excessively withdrawn or timid children may not get referred as these problems do not cause concern for the school or may not even be noticed. It is possible that the EBD problems experienced by girls tend to fall into this category. Therefore when LEAs proceed with a statutory assessment of a child who may be EBD one is tempted to conclude that it is the school and not necessarily the child and his or her family that is being helped.

A Framework for the Assessment of Children with Emotional and Behavioural Difficulties

Despite the voluminous literature going back many years on causes, definition and treatment approaches for children who have emotional and behavioural problems, very little has been written about how to assess these children, Hoghughi (1992) being a notable exception. Recently Faupel (1990) and Wood *et al.* (1993) have provided some guidelines and McCall and Farrell (1993) have reported on approaches used by educational psychologists. In view of the problems in arriving at an acceptable definition of the term it is perhaps not surprising that few guidelines on how to conduct assessments exist. In the remainder of this chapter I describe how staff can use a structured framework to guide their assessments which can help to ensure that all parties are properly consulted and involved, that all aspects of the child's behaviour and the social contexts are considered and that a range of assessment methods are used. Throughout it is important to be sensitive to and aware of the issues that can arise as these children may be very distressed and/or cause distress for others. Parents may blame the school for the problem and vice versa. The whole assessment process can be emotionally charged and in this climate calmness and sympathetic approaches are essential.

When assessing child who has been referred because of his/her emotional and behavioural problems there are two broad aspects to consider, the *parameters of the problem* and the *range of assessment methods* which could be used.

Parameters of the Problem

These can be divided as follows.

History of the problem

Have the child's problems persisted over time, what form have they taken; when did they start; how have they developed? What intervention methods have been tried and with what result?

In what settings does the problem occur?

Does the problem occur at home and at school or just in one setting? Are the behaviours similar or different in each setting? Are there more problems in certain lessons or in the playground? Does the problem only occur in the presence of specific individuals, for example one or other of the parents/ guardians, certain teachers or specific groups of children?

What are the child's relationships with parents/guardians, teachers, siblings, peers?

As discussed earlier failure to form meaningful and fulfilling relationships is one of the factors associated with emotional and behavioural difficulties. It is therefore important to assess how the child views the relationship with the important people in his/her life.

What are the parents/guardians, teachers, siblings and peers relationships with the child?

It is also important to assess what other people feel about the child. For example do they accept of reject the child, do they like or are they frightened by the child, do they try to avoid being with him or her? This applies to all people with whom the child has regular contact.

The child's self-image

This is crucial to overall adjustment. How does the child feel about himself/ herself. For example does he/she feel inadequate, insecure, a failure and unable to cope? Alternatively is the child's self-image totally unrealistic and out of touch with reality? For example he/she may feel capable of attaining goals which are completely beyond his/her ability and suggest that he/she is living in something of a fantasy world.

The child's view of the problem

Does the child view the problem in the same way or differently from others. What are his/her feelings (for example, depression, anger, unhappiness), is he/she in control of them? Does he/she display any insight into the causes of the problem? Does the child genuinely wish to change?

Assessing the extent of the problem by looking at each of these parameters helps to ensure that the assessment covers all the important areas. In general:

- if the problem is prevalent across all settings and with all the people with whom the child has contact;
- if it has persisted for some time (at least a year) in each of these settings and with all these people despite any intervention that has been offered;
- if the child's self-image is poor or totally unrealistic;
- if the child's feelings about the problem reveal him/her to be extremely unhappy or distressed and not in control of his/her emotions;

then there is evidence that the child's problems may be so severe as to warrant extra resources being made available in the form of a statement. However for many children who may be initially described as having EBD an assessment may reveal that, for example, the problem is only evident with a few teachers in specific settings or that apart from teachers, the child has made good relationships and has many friends. Such children may indeed pose considerable problems for their teachers or parents for which an intervention programme should be planned, but to say that they have emotional and behavioural difficulties would be an inaccurate and exaggerated description of their problems. Similarly there are many children who truant from school or who are labelled as delinquent who are perfectly well adjusted and should not be described as having EBD. Psychologists and behavioural support teachers can sometimes come under pressure to attach the label EBD when an analysis of the problem which examines all the parameters listed above would not lead to that conclusion.

Assessment Methods

The parameters of the problem reflect the wide range of areas which need to be investigated. When carrying out an investigation it is important to use a variety of assessment methods each of which can focus on a number of the parameters. These are discussed below.

Reports from child, parents teachers and others

This is a key part of an assessment. Those involved are often showered with written and verbal reports from many sources. Often several teachers reports are better than one as they may paint a different picture of the child. Reports should be analyzed for evidence of discrepancies and congruence. It is also important not to take all reports at face value. There may be hidden agendas and subtle and not immediately obvious reasons why certain things were said or not said.

Direct observation of the behaviour

This could be structured observation of a child in a number of settings using an specified observation technique. It is more likely to be done by a behavioural support teacher or an educational psychologist. Usually there is insufficient time to observe the child in every setting but it helps outside agencies to get a better view of the problem if they have actually observed the child in a setting in which it normally occurs. Too often educational psychologists and behavioural support teachers just hear about a problem without directly observing it.

Collaborative interviews and discussions

These could be between teachers, parents educational psychologists, support teachers or any combination of these. They go beyond simple verbal reports and may include, for example, counselling the parents in an attempt to reassure them or some exchange of information which can lead to a better understanding of the causes of the problem, for example, if a child changed class or a relative has died.

Clinical assessment

This is hard to define but relates to clinical judgments made by the teachers, educational psychologists, support workers on the extent or cause of the problem and on what to do about it. Clinical judgment depends on the interpretation of such factors as what is said or not said, body language, eye contact. This is the most personal part of the assessment and interpretation may depend on the professional's own theoretical beliefs and training about emotional and behavioural difficulties.

Tests and rating scales

There is no shortage of such instruments that can be used to assess a child who may have emotional and behavioural difficulties. Rating scales such as the Bristol Social Adjustment Guides or the Rutter Scales have been widely used for research purposes but not commonly employed as a tool to assessing children with EBD. Other 'tests' of personality are used even less frequently possibly because they have not reached the degree of 'objectivity' and international respectability that traditional tests of attainment and ability have acquired. However with appropriate training some psychologists can apply these tests effectively.

Interventions over time

In order to complete a thorough assessment further information can be gained by planning an intervention programme, implementing it carefully and evaluating the outcome. The success or otherwise of an intervention programme provides further information about the nature of the problem and can lead to a more accurate prediction of the possible long-term outcome.

In summary the more assessment methods used the more certain we can be about the accuracy of the assessment. Simply relying on the reports from one source, for example parents or teachers may give a distorted picture. On receipt of a damming report from the school, a behavioural support teacher or educational psychologist may feel under pressure to make recommendations which might may lead the LEA to draw up a statement and it is therefore vitally important to use other sources of data to confirm or reject the teachers' reports before reaching a conclusion. Similarly it would be unwise to rely solely on clinical judgment or the results of a psychological test before making a decision about a child.

This framework for assessing children with EBD can be represented on a grid (see figure 1.1) which makes it possible to see how the parameters of a problem can be associated with the assessment methods used although this is clearly not possible for each parameter and assessment method. For example although people's reports about a child's can refer to all the parameters, tests and rating scales are likely to focus on the child relationship and on his/her self-esteem. The model can be used as a grid or checklist so that when coming to a conclusion about a child's problems it is possible to check that all possible assessment methods have been used and that all problem parameters have been investigated.

Finally, it is important to remember that assessment is a dynamic and ongoing process and, particularly for the class teacher or SENCO, doesn't have a clear cut beginning. Initial assessment may lead to some form of intervention the results of which provide further important assessment information which guides the next stage in the assessment process. Assessment and intervention are therefore cyclical and this is in line with the staged model of assessment described in the Code of Practice.

Conclusion

The concept of emotional and behavioural difficulties is complex and ill-defined. Children who are labelled as EBD frequently experience feelings of rejection and hostility from parents and teachers who may also be equally distressed by the situation. Children tend to come from the socially and economically disadvantaged families where parents feel disempowered and have problems working effectively with teachers and other professionals. Those who work in this field need to be sensitive to these issues and to recognize that they themselves and the way they interact with the pupil may also be part of the problem.

Figure 1.1: *Framework for assessing children who may have emotional and behavioural difficulties*

Assessment methods

Parameters of the problem	Reports (written/verbal)			Observation	Interviews/ discussions	Clinical Assessment	Tests/Rating Scales	Intervention over time
	Ch	Sch	Ps	Other					
History of problem									
Settings: Home School Community									
Child's relationships with: Teachers Peers Parents Siblings									
Others relationships with child: Teachers Peers Parents Siblings									
Self-image: Poor unrealistic									
Child's view of problem									

In an attempt to unravel some of the issues in this complex area this chapter has briefly reviewed the causes and definition of the term emotional and behavioural difficulties and has suggested a framework which can guide our assessment so as to help us make informed and rational decisions about these vulnerable children.

References

CANTER, L. and CANTER, M. (1992) *Assertive Discipline: Positive Management for Today's Classrooms*, Bristol, Behaviour Management Ltd.

CHISHOLM, B., KEARNEY, D., KNIGHT, G., LITTLE, H., MORRIS, S. and TWEDDLE, D. (1986) *Preventative Approaches to Disruption*, London, Macmillan Education.

COOPER, P. (1993) *Effective Schools for Disaffected Students*, London, Routledge.

DFE (1993) *Education for Disaffected Pupils*, London, Department for Education Publications Centre.

DFE (1994) *Code of Practice on the Identification and Assessment of Special Educational Needs*, London, Department for Education Publications Centre.

DFE (1994) *Circulars on Pupils with Problems*, London, Department for Education Publications Centre.

FAUPEL, A. (1990) 'A model response to emotional and behavioural development in schools', *Educational Psychology in Practice*, **5**, 4, pp. 172–83.

GALVIN, P., MERCER, S. and COSTA, P. (1990) *Building a Better Behaved School*, Longman.

HERBERT, M. (1993) *Working with Children and the Children Act*, London, British Psychological Society.

HOGHUGHI, M. (1992) *Assessing Child and Adolescent Disorders*, London, Sage Publications.

HOUGHTON, S., WHELDALL, K. and MERRETT, F. (1988) 'Classroom behaviour problems which secondary school teachers find most troublesome', *British Educational Research Journal*, **14**, 3, pp. 297–312.

MCCALL, L. and FARRELL, P. (1993) 'Methods used by educational psychologists to assess children with emotional and behavioural problems', *Educational Psychology in Practice*, **9**, 3, pp. 164–170.

MALCOLM, L. and HADDOCK, L. (1992) ' "Make trouble get results", provision for girls in the support services', *Educational Psychology in Practice*, **8**, 2, pp. 97–102.

REID, J. (1987) 'A problem in the family, explanations under strain' in BOOTH T. and COULBY D. (Eds) *Producing and Reducing Disaffection*, Milton Keynes, Open University Press.

REYNOLDS, D. and SULLIVAN, M. (1981) 'The effects of schools, a radical faith re-stated', in GILLHAM B. (Ed) *Problem Behaviour in the Secondary School*, London, Croom Helm.

RUTTER, M., MAUGHAN, B., MORTIMORE, P. and OUSTON, J. (1979) *Fifteen Thousand Hours: Secondary Schools and their Effects on Children*, London, Open Books.

UPTON, G. (1992) 'No time for complacency', *Special Children*, July, pp. 23–7.

WHELDALL, K. and MERRETT, F. (1989a) *Positive Teaching in the Secondary School*, London, Paul Chapman Publishing.

WHELDALL, K. and MERRETT, F (1989b) *Positive Teaching in the Primary School*, London, Paul Chapman Publishing.

WOOD, D., GOTT, J. and JAMES, D. (1993) 'EBD — criteria or aide memoire?', *Educational Psychology in Practice*, **9**, 3, pp. 156–64.

Chapter 2

Different Perspectives of Parents and Educational Psychologists when a Child is Referred for EBD Assessment

Nick Boreham, Ian Peers, Peter Farrell and Denise Craven

Introduction

One of the main aims of the 1981 and 1993 Education Acts has been to encourage parents to take an active part in the assessment of their children who might have special educational needs. Parents have been given rights to be present at assessments, to make written contributions, to seek the advice of other professionals not nominated by the LEA and to appeal against decisions made. They also have access to all professionals' reports. The whole ethos is one of seeing parents as equal partners in the assessment process. The legislation reflects the impact of several writers who have stressed the vital importance of fully involving parents in all aspects of their child's education (see, for example, Wolfendale, 1985 and 1992; Mittler and McConachie, 1983). Indeed for many years it has been the view of the present government that parents should play a greater part in planning and shaping their children's education. Unfortunately since the implementation of the 1981 Act there has been growing concern that parents have not felt that they were working in genuine partnership with other professionals. For example very few use the opportunity offered by the Act to write their own views about their child despite the efforts of Wolfendale (1985) and others to make it easier for them to do so. The complex appeals procedures may have left parents feeling they were fighting a losing battle particularly as so many appeals have been unsuccessful. Time will tell if the tribunal system introduced as part of the 1993 Act will improve matters in this regard. See Farrell (1988) for a more detailed discussion of the issues. Marks (1991) has studied 1981 Act case conference reviews and in her analysis of communications between mothers and professionals she reported that ambiguities and mothers' uncertainties were denied in favour of promoting a united professional front.

Whilst recent education legislation and many LEA policies on referrals aspire to a participative decision-making approach, de facto they appear to operate a political or arena model of decision making (Bacharach and Lawler, 1986). Too often the LEAs need to keep within its budget and resources may override the assessed needs of the child and the wishes of the parents. As Farrell (1989) argues, educational psychologists (EPs) are inexorably bound up in this process and, as LEA employees, may feel under pressure to make recommendations which are in line with the current LEA practice and not work as an independent advocate for the child and family. This may influence the way they relate with parents when undertaking an assessment.

This chapter explores this issue by reporting on an exploratory study of ten cases referred to a Schools Psychological Service on the grounds of emotional and behavioural difficulty (EBD). One of the main aims of the study was to explore differences in the way EPs and parents view the situation following a referral. Prior to the responding to the referral, the EP contacted the family to seek their permission to take part in the study. Having gained their agreement, the researcher (Denise Craven) interviewed the EPs, parents, children, headteachers, class teachers and learning support teachers on successive occasions over a six-month period, as each case progressed towards resolution. She also observed the EPs' interviews with parents, children, headteachers and other teachers involved with special needs. Most of the interviews were audio-recorded, while others were written up as fully as possible afterwards. The average interview/observation lasted fifty minutes and a total of sixty-four interviews and case conferences were observed. The method of collecting data was similar to that used by Armstrong *et al.* (1991) although a different range of issues were explored.

None of the cases resulted in a statement of special educational need, although the EPs' expectations had initially been that several would go as far as that. In the event, most cases were resolved by the EP working with the school or the parents to allay anxieties and to improve behaviour management techniques. The fact that during the six-month period of the study none of the children were statemented is surprising in view of McCall and Farrell's (1993) finding that out of fifty-seven cases in their study, forty-one were statemented. One possible reason for this difference might have been that we were not given access to the more problematic cases in view of the intrusive nature of the method of data collection. The whole process of being assessed as having an emotional and behavioural problem is understandably traumatic for many parents and children and the additional presence of a researcher may have been perceived by the EPs to possibly jeopardize the smooth progress of the assessment. EPs may have therefore only offered referrals for us to study which did not appear to be too 'serious'. It is, of course, possible that after the study was completed some of the children may have ended up being statemented. However the absence of 'statemented assessments' and indeed psychiatric illness and other pathologies from the sample should be borne in mind when interpreting the EPs' actions.

Nick Boreham, Ian Peers, Peter Farrell and Denise Craven

Distributed Decisions

A Theoretical Model

Although there is a widespread assumption that multi-agent decisions can only be made on the basis of shared understanding, in practice much decision-making is distributed. The term 'distributed' refers to the constraint when the decision-making network does not have a common view of the problem (Rasmussen *et al.*, *1991*). The result is that members have to coordinate their action on the basis of partial and even conflicting views. This is a promising conceptual framework for analyzing decision making by multidisciplinary teams in a wide range of social and educational contexts. The basic hypothesis in the present study is that, despite the customary channels of communication between parents and professionals, they are attempting to collaborate on the basis of inconsistent models of the problem.

The interpretative framework is provided by the notion of *situational awareness* (SA). This refers to how well the individual is keeping track of the train of events so that he/she can select an appropriate course of action. A more detailed definition of SA includes the following three properties:

- perception of elements: what details of the objective situation are actually perceived by the individual;
- information integration: How this information is synthesized into a meaningful whole;
- projection of future states: What may happen in the future.

For the purposes of this chapter, we focus on the differences between the EPs' and parents' situational awareness in the early stages of working with the cases. The purpose is to develop a definition of SA suitable for analyzing data on EBD assessments, and to explore barriers to communication at this crucial stage in the assessment procedure.

Analysis

The interviews were transcribed on to disk for analysis by the qualitative data analysis package *The Ethnograph*. Segments of text revealing situational awareness by EPs and parents were coded and collated. As this was an exploratory analysis, data from the different cases were pooled into one EP set and one parent set. Each set was then sub-divided by the SA triad of perception of elements, information integration and projection of future states. Finally, comparisons were made between the EPs and parents on each of these dimensions.

Psychologists' Situational Awareness

All the EPs constructed a model of the case by drawing on prior knowledge and by collecting new information. This process continued as the EP interacted with other participants. However, these interactions were not simply used as a means of data collection, but as opportunities for influencing other people's expectations.

Perception of Elements

We found three significant aspects of the way the EPs perceived the elements of the cases: reliance on prior knowledge of the school, scepticism about information sources, and seeing through attempts to sway their judgment.

Prior knowledge of the school

Most EPs were able to go beyond the information given in the referral form on the basis of their prior knowledge of how schools in general handle cases of EBD, and even by knowing the individual school that had made the referral. For example in the following two cases:

> *EP:* There is a strong possibility they will have tried sort of various unsystematic normal disciplinary things like shouting at him or telling him off or making him sit somewhere else . . .

> *EP:* . . . well, they might do it a little bit, but it is actually quite, well knowing the particular school it's unlikely that they will now be ready to do very much em, . . . uh, we may have to look at doing Section 5 assessment.

Scepticism about information sources

As they began to gather information, the EPs clearly regarded some sources of information as less reliable than others. As one EP put it when interviewed after a meeting with teachers:

> *EP:* . . . I was having to sort of think whether the information we were being given by people in school was worth fourpence, the head doesn't teach that kid, so he doesn't know, he only knows what other people have said to him . . .

> *EP:* . . . the teacher we talked to is a stand in supply teacher . . . and was probably under a lot of pressure and so had a very jaundiced view . . .

Seeing through attempts to sway their judgment

The EPs demonstrated a ready capacity to perceive hidden motives. For example:

> *INT*:   The Head actually, if you remember, made reference to already having one statemented child in that class em, the second time we were chatting.
>
> *EP*:   Yea that's, that's a manoeuvre to say, there's already one bad one in there we can't keep another one like this without some more help, that's what that means.

Another EP used the metaphor of 'tokens' to describe a headteacher's way of describing a case:

> *EP*:   Well that's just a turn of phrase, em if you actually analyze what the head says it's in fact a series of educational tokens and they don't really mean anything about of the individual kid. He trots out his tokens em, so I don't listen to that . . .
>
>   . . . so, so what he goes for is an account of Paul's behaviour that's in the sort of terms that, that he thinks I might be em, able to accept, and em, and they (the terms) were, he's very attention seeking and em, a number of the sort standard tokens that are used to carry on these conversations in staff rooms, in fact em, I don't think they form any coherent theoretical analysis of what's up with Paul at all or are of any help whatsoever in doing anything about Paul, but you know, that's the exchange rate, that's what we work in, so he gave me all the right counters, poor concentration, short attention span, poor short term memory, em, and all the usual stuff you see that's meant to be an explanation of what Paul is doing, em and, and in exchange for that I provide some help, tuition time, 'cause that's what all that's worth, em, and, and if that happens then that's fine as far as the Head's concerned 'cause then the teacher will stop coming to his office, and saying, 'Hell Paul . . .'

Information Integration

The EPs had little difficulty in forming an integrated situational assessment. We found two significant ways in which they integrated case details into a meaningful whole: diagnostic and temporal conceptual frameworks.

Diagnostic framework

In their initial interviews, the EPs revealed tight bipolar constructs for classifying referrals. Three of these recurred frequently: a serious vs a routine/nuisance case; a problem arising within the education system vs a problem arising 'within the family'; and a behavioural problem vs a learning difficulty. This classification system enabled the EPs to chunk information and process it efficiently.

Serious EBD problems were construed as cases where other helping professions were already involved, or where it was thought they should be involved. One EP when asked by the interviewer about a forthcoming assessment commented:

> *EP*:   . . . I mean obviously funny things may come up like you know it suddenly turns out to be a major thing that actually he is being seen by the paediatrician for something . . .
>
> . . . or if he is already being seen by the family counselling service and they have been at it for some time.

-another suggested 'serious problems' are those which are likely to necessitate interagency collaboration:

> *EP*:   . . . where the other adults can't deal with it very easily it may be more appropriate to ask another agency to work with the family over a more extended period.

These comments reveal boundary conditions for the seriousness of the problem. At the 'routine' pole of the serious-routine construct were notions such as the following:

> *EP*:   . . . on the face of it, there is um, the school there, is in effect saying we have run out of things to stop this child from behaving in ways we don't approve of for some reason, and we would like your advice about what to do next.

EPs often located the problem within the education system:

> *EP*:   Em, well it's a problem for the teachers really at this stage, it's a problem for the teacher's in terms of em, they, whatever they are doing they are unable to control him.

At the other end of the dimension, problems construed as 'within family' were often seen from an interactionist perspective:

> *EP*:   Absolutely, yes, I believe that children with problems the roots are interpersonal in terms of a child's relationships how they feel about themselves, how they view the world, how they view other people treating them.

The following illustrates how cases could be classified as either 'behaviour' or 'learning':

> *EP*: . . . so that I mean because he's a behaviour one, I know this sounds terrible, because he's a behaviour one, he's likely to get more of my time than if he was a learning one, a learning one they're nice and neat, well they're not always but you know, they're neater, you know, you can get hold of it quicker and you can make a decision, I guess a rather more informed decision maybe rather quicker than you can with behaviour one's.

This comment clearly indicates that this EP thought it was harder to make an accurate assessment of a child with EBD than it was for a child with learning difficulties.

Temporal framework

EPs also construed details in their temporal context. In the first case meeting with a headteacher in a school, the following EP asks for information to help position the referral temporally:

> *EP*: Has there been any improvement since being here?
> *HT*: Seems to be less report of violent behaviour, he seems to have grown out of this . . .
> . . . He's difficult to talk to, you get a yes/no response. He's totally switched off when being reprimanded he's been there before so he switches off . . .

This type of exchange allows the EP to rapidly establish an integrated picture. An example from the same case where the EP is meeting for the first time with a parent is:

> *EP*: Is he any different from two/three years ago?
> *PAR*: No not really, he's not so destructive at home apart from his bedroom, he wrecks his bedroom and ignores his toys.
> *EP*: Have things changed since starting school?
> *PAR*: Mrs . . . (current teacher) complains more, she seems more highly strung than Mrs . . . (previous nursery teacher). Mrs . . . (current teacher) seems to complain about everything, even what might be normal child behaviour.

Construing events within temporal frameworks adds to their significance and is characteristic of expert thinking in general.

Projection of Future States

The EPs made clear projections of future actions and goals. In respect of the cases sampled here, they regarded their role as helping the schools to handle

the disturbance and return to homeostasis. While the responsibility for decid-
ing action is the EP's, the overall task of bringing the system into harmony
again is achieved by allocating sub-tasks to others. We use the term 'system
fixer' to describe this perception:

> *EP*:   . . . are unable to control him so that he gets on with his work
> and doesn't cause everybody a lot of trouble so em, if I can help
> it's going to be helping them to manage his behaviour more
> effectively.

This role is exemplified by another EP when describing his intentions for a
case:

> *EP*:   . . . being realistic, um, I am not thinking of and have no real
> intentions of doing any kind of therapeutic work I know I won't
> have time to do that, that's sort of ruled out so it has basically
> got to be some kind of administrative fix of one kind or another.

This comment also illustrates the influence of resource constraints (in this case
— time) on the EP's thinking. Two other EPs, one in describing the purpose
of an assessment, and another in considering what she might put in her report,
commented thus:

> *EP*:   I mean the purpose I suppose is to hope in some way that I can
> help them get round the problem they're having with this child
> as I say by either managing the behaviour or moving him
> somewhere else.

> *EP*:   I shall say that I see it as a management problem and lay out
> some general principles for managing his behaviour and the sort
> of things to try to aim for and to try to avoid other things.

Thus the average EP's projection in these 'routine' cases is not based on a
psychological diagnosis, or allocation of fault and responsibility, but on a
pragmatic schema for affecting system adjustments to accommodate disturbances. The search for more information stops when a way of influencing the
current state of the system towards homeostasis is found. Solutions considered
are likely to be those which have worked in the past and are consistent with
policy and resource availability. The EP quoted above would not consider
therapeutic work with a child because of the time demand. In another example an EP comments:

> *EP*:   . . . just that I can't really do anything about internal life in the
> amount of space that I've got available, — but I can probably do

something about, or get the teacher to do something about how that manifests itself on the outside.

As another commented, the criterion of success is 'keeping the school happy'.

Parents' Situational Awareness

Like the EPs, parents attempted to construct a model of the situation, but unlike them they did not have a method of tactical thinking. Information was often sought from parents but not shared with them. They had to actively seek out information and they did not feel confident in doing this. Their initial situational assessment could be characterized as fragmented, incomplete, and sometimes internally inconsistent. This was not helped by feelings of anxiety. Parents appeared to use an attributional framework in which their children's behaviour could only be explained by causes. Their immediate concerns could be described as seeking these causes and specific advice on the cures.

Perception of Elements

We found four significant aspects of the parents' perception of elements. Unlike the EPs, their situational assessments showed *lack of information*; acceptance of information at *face value*; focus on *defect in the child or family*; and focus on *blame — mainly of themselves.*

Lack of information

In one case, following meetings with the headteacher in school, and a post-assessment meeting with an EP, the parent was still confused and had incomplete information about the situation:

> *PAR*: I don't really know why he was referred, all we were doing were getting reports from school that he was being a naughty child, like he wouldn't sit down, I mean we had reports he was going to run out of school and . . . answering one of his teachers back, I don't know which teacher it was, he wasn't like that at the Grange school he was no worse than other kids.

To improve their situational awareness, parents attempted to elicit information from the LEA, the school, and even the interviewer (which presented an interesting ethical dilemma illustrated in the following dialogue with parents):

> *INT*: Right, can I ask you when you actually made the first referral?'
> *PAR*: Em, it was before Christmas, it would be something like November . . .

INT: So it was November?

PAR: Yes it would be.

INT: So five months ago since your first contact?

PAR: Yea . . .

INT: So when did you write the (second) letter?

PAR: I'm just trying to think, it'd be January I think, I've probably got a note of that in my diary actually.

INT: I was going to ask you what did you get back then from the psychological services?

PAR: Nothing.

INT: Nothing at all?

PAR: No.

INT: Not a letter?

PAR: No.

INT: You didn't get a little leaflet?

PAR: No, nothing at all.

INT: Do you know anything about the possibilities, you know, what might happen as a result of the assessment?

PAR: No I don't know . . . Are *you* going to tell us?

In another case, the mother described a typical response when she approached the school for information:

PAR: Yea, whereas if I went to the teacher they tend to say well you'll have to see what Mrs (EP) says, they don't ever give me the straight answer that I want.

Face value

In sharp contrast to the EPs' ability to see through what they were being told, the parents tended to take information at face value:

PAR: Well, to be honest when they tell me he goes to a special school I got it in my mind, I've got an opinion if they, if they say he's got to go to a school, then he must because they know.

Defect in the child or family

In contrast to the EPs' focus on system problems, the parents' situational awareness frequently focused on supposed defects in the child or family. They were often seeking a causal explanation in terms of the medical model:

PAR: . . . just give him an x-ray and if it was cloudy or something it might give you, you know, at least then you've eliminated another process . . .

Or they often had an expectation that the EP could effect a 'cure':

> PAR: . . . when I asked him specifically what he would be doing in order to cure the problem he didn't seem to be able to tell me any concrete suggestions.

Blame — *mainly of themselves*

This attributional framework led the parents to blame themselves. Feelings of self doubt, denial and concern were evident when the interviewer asked the following parent what she thought about her son seeing the EP:

> PAR: I'm not sure — no, I'm a bit dubious of why, at the moment I have my doubts . . . I know myself personally that he's not slow, but something in the back of my mind somebody's trying to tell me along the lines something is wrong you know . . .

In the absence of a clear situational awareness, the parent searches for an explanation of the apparent problems and attributes them to herself:

> PAR: I'm saying he's just like me so it's all my fault, my Dad says you can't expect pears off apple trees, that it, you know what you can expect.

Even when parents were provided with an explanation for the problematic behaviour in terms of a system problem (for example, 'this child has a nuisance value for that teacher') or when they were provided with reassurance (for example, 'he's growing up and going through a sticky patch'), they often still tended to blame the family or themselves:

> PAR: I've done something wrong for him to be like that, yea, I always think what did I do wrong? — but I can't place what I did wrong because I've never done owt wrong, yes in me mind I'm thinking, well when he was a baby what did I do wrong, you know?

Information Integration

In contrast with the EPs, the parents lacked a conceptual framework for integrating information. An example of an internally contradictory view of the situation is that of the following parent (already partially quoted above):

> PAR: I don't really know why he was referred, all we were doing were getting reports from school that he was being a naughty child, like he wouldn't sit down, I mean we had reports he was

going to run out of school and . . . answering one of his teachers back, I don't know which teacher it was, he wasn't like that at the Grange School where he was no worse than other kids.

Further statements from this parent, not reported here, reveal that her initial perception was that her child was 'no worse than other kids'. Her conclusion from the comments quoted above was that the 'teacher actually had a problem'. The actual referral to the EP followed a period in which there had been no communication from the school, 'I've had no further reports'. She then began to doubt her own reasoning and came to the conclusion that the problem was not within the school but within David.

Projection of Future States

This dimension of the parents' situational awareness demonstrated a marked contrast with that of the EPs. The main constituents of the parents' image of the future were confusion and fear of their child going to a special school:

> *PAR*:　. . . he said that he would have to be removed and go to a special school. I don't think he meant a special school or a special what do you call unit, a special unit.

This parent's expectations were imprecise:

> *PAR*:　What do I think is going to happen — I can't see anything is going to happen really, just discussing it, talking . . . it's just talking at the moment nothing is being done. I mean I can't really say what's going to be done you know.

In the following case there was a clear contrast between the EP's situational awareness and that of the parents. The EP commented:

> *EP*:　I think very often, the role of the EP is to let the school feel that they're doing something and let time go by and let the kid survive and grow through the difficult patch.

Yet in the same case the parents' situational awareness after the child had been assessed by the EP could be summed up as mixed feelings of contradiction and helplessness:

> *PAR*:　I was worried about whether they'd throw him out or whatever — well, whenever I talked to the headmaster he sort of chews it away as if it's not that important, you know, we're only letting you know how bad he is we're not actually that worried about it.

> . . . I've tried to get help myself and I'm getting nowhere. . . . until the problems sorted then I'm going to be anxious because you never know when they are going to suddenly say 'well enough's enough'.

Parents were deeply concerned about the consequences:

> INT: So what's the worst thing that might happen for you then?'
> PAR: I suppose it's going to a special school but my mother in law says to me when I told her, 'well why, you shouldn't be ashamed of your son', she tells me this, 'why is it that you don't want him to go to a special school is it cos you're ashamed of what other people might say'. I said, 'well that's partly', but the main reason is like I say every Mother wants her child to be good at school, you know I mean I wasn't brilliant at school but I did exams . . .

As another parent poignantly asked:

> PAR: If he did go to special school, have you known anybody to get a good job after it?

Discussion

The main conclusion of this study is that the EPs and parents in the cases studied frequently commenced the assessment procedure with inconsistent views of the situation.

The EPs developed a clear situational awareness early in the case. While they aspired to a child-centred role, their actual priority in these cases was conflict resolution and returning stability to the system. The intervention they anticipated making was to adjust the school's behaviour to accommodate the disturbance, removing the child being viewed as a last resort. Consequently, their initial attention tended to focus on the system rather than on the child and his/her parents.

In contrast, the parents demonstrated a very confused situational awareness. Their knowledge base was minimal, their anxiety high, they needed concrete information and advice, yet they had no definite strategy for information seeking. In contrast to the system-level thinking of the EP, parents tended to see the problem in terms of the medical model and were looking for the cause (in the child or family) and possibly a cure. They feared exclusion from mainstream school and the stigma attached to special schools.

There are clear implications for improving professional practice which follow from this study. We shall focus on two; implications for improving EPs' assessment techniques and for improving the quality of parental involvement.

Implications for EPs

As stated above, the results of this study suggest that EPs in the particular range of cases included in the sample see themselves as helping schools to manage their pupils more effectively. Indeed, they may be successful in achieving this aim as none of the pupils in this sample were transferred to a special school. They are 'system fixers' working within the limits of their own time and resources and those of the LEA.

The Code of Practice (DFE, 1994) lays down specific criteria to guide professional decision making on the full range of special needs, including children with EBD. Although these refer to information required prior to referral for statutory assessment, they clearly relate to assessment strategies that all professionals should adopt, including EPs, when working with these children. The guidelines in the Code suggest that professionals should consider within child factors such as ability, attainment and personality, the child's ability to form relationships and specific behaviour difficulties, for example, eating disorders, school refusal, bullying. In addition the results of the school's attempts to help the child so far should also form part of the assessment. Surprisingly no mention is made of the relevance of assessing the child relationship with his or her family. The Code therefore stresses within child and situational factors in the school as being important for assessing EBD and it is interesting that despite the fact that the pupils in this study were seen before the onset of the Code, these were the areas on which the EPs focused. However we do not think that this necessarily means that EPs practice was exemplary. There was only limited evidence that their work was informed by theory. Furthermore, as one of the key professionals involved in EBD assessment, and as probably the only ones to have received specific training in this area, it would not be unreasonable to expect the level of work to have extended beyond that of a 'system fixer'. EPs have a responsibility to develop their assessment practices in this vitally important area such that they can offer a truly *psychological* assessment.

Implications for Parental Involvement

The EPs seemed to be relatively clear about what was happening. The same could not be said of the parents. On the whole they were confused, sometimes blaming themselves for what had happened and extremely worried about the outcome of the assessment. In no sense did they perceive themselves to be equal partners; things were being done to them over which they had little control. The intentions of the 1981 Act and all the government circulars which superseded it do not seem to have improved the situation at all.

The extent of the problem of making parents equal partners in the assessment process is revealed by the finding that, despite the customary contact between them, the situational awareness of many parents was inconsistent with that of the EPs. When decision-making is distributed in this sense, the kind of partnership envisaged by the 1981 and 1993 Acts is impossible. Yet the solution is not just to 'inform the parents', for example, give them a leaflet or write a letter about some proposed action. The differences in situational awareness that created such a gulf between the EPs and the parents were deep-rooted, arising from differences in the background knowledge they brought with them to the task. The EPs training and professional experience had clearly left them cognitively well equipped for perceiving important facts, integrating them into a significant picture and predicting the likely course of events. In contrast, the diffuse, inaccurate and self-derogatory perceptions of the parents may be attributed to their lack of background knowledge which comes with professional training and experience. This was their first case of an EBD referral, and they lacked the cognitive framework necessary for construing such features of the situation and its 'seriousness' and whether the problem was located in the family or the educational system itself. It is hardly surprising they struggled with little success to make sense of what was happening. Lacking background knowledge needed to transform the information they received into effective situational awareness, they constructed meanings out of the alternative conceptual frameworks which were available to them. In the present case, these consisted of self doubt, fears of unpredictable authorities powerful enough to take their children away from them, and a crude folk-psychology with its implications of the need for a 'cure' of the imagined 'defect'. The findings of this study demonstrate that professionals cannot take it for granted that parents understand what is happening in EBD assessment just because they have been informed. Many parents will lack the cognitive framework needed to make sense of what they are told. Empowering them as full partners in the assessment process requires more to be done about this level of their understanding.

Acknowledgement

We are grateful for the help and support of Peter Mittler, Professor of Special Education at the University of Manchester, who participated in this study and commented on early drafts of the chapter.

References

ARMSTRONG, D., GALLOWAY, D. and TOMLINSON, S. (1991) 'Decision-making in psychologists' professional interviews', *Educational Psychology in Practice*, **7**, 2, pp. 82–7.
BACHARACH, S.B. and LAWLER, E.J. (1986) 'Power dependence and power paradoxes in bargaining', *Negotiation Journal*, **2**, pp. 167–74.
DFE (1994) *Education Act 1993: Code of Practice on the Identification and Assessment of Special Educational Needs*, London, DFE Publications Centre.

FARRELL, P. (1988) 'Education policy, legislation and implementation' in LEIGHTON, A. (Ed) *Mental Handicap in the Community*, Woodhead-Faulkner.

FARRELL, P. (1989) 'Educational psychology services: Crisis or opportunity', *The Psychologist*, **12**, 6, pp. 240–1.

McCALL, L. and FARRELL, P. (1993) 'Methods used by educational psychologists to assess children with emotional and behavioural difficulties', *Educational Psychology in Practice*, **9**, 3, pp. 164–70.

MARKS, D.S. (1991) 'Talking to mothers: Rhetoric and practice within education case conferences', *British Psychological Society, Division of Educational and Child Psychology Newsletter*, **46**, pp. 24–9.

MITTLER, P. and McCONACHIE, H. (1983) (Eds) *Parents, Professionals and Mentally Handicapped People: Approaches to Partnership*, London, Croom Helm.

RASMUSSEN, J., BREHMER, B. and LEPLAT, J. (Eds) (1991) *Distributed Decision Making, Cognitive Models for Cooperative Work*, New York, John Wiley.

WOLFENDALE, S. (1985) 'Parental profiling and the parental contribution to Section 5 (Education Act 1981) assessment and statementing procedures', *Newsletter of the Association for Child Psychology and Child Psychiatry*, **7**, 2, pp. 16–19.

WOLFENDALE, S. (1992) *Empowering Parents and Teachers: Working for Children*, London, Cassell.

Chapter 3

Emotional and Behavioural Difficulties: The Primary School Experience

Eric Peagam

Few today would deny that concerns, about children's emotional and (more particularly) behavioural difficulties rank high with teachers, and that this has been so for some time. Debates about the role of the school and curriculum in originating and sustaining these difficulties, have made it possible to state, as Lund (1990) has, that:

> most workers now see the child's difficulties as a function of inappropriate curriculum content and this view has been strengthened by the Elton Report. (p. 75)

Furthermore, in spite of the movement (among theoreticians at least) away from 'within-child' explanations of disturbed and disturbing behaviour, there remains a feeling on the part of many teachers that such explanations deny the reality of their daily experience, and, in so doing, invalidate the strategies and expertise that they have developed to address these realities. There is also considerable evidence that these concerns are now more than ever affecting teachers in primary schools so that, in spite of the increasing use of whole-school behaviour policies and structured approaches to discipline, there has been a significant rise both in the numbers of children being excluded, and those being referred for special education as a result of emotional and behavioural difficulties.

This study reported in this chapter was therefore conceived in an attempt to examine and assess the scale of these difficulties; and to seek common features among the children concerned and the schools in which they were found. It was carried out in a single large, urban LEA and although, inevitably, each LEA had its own particular experience and developed its own responses, many issues were common to all of them so that some useful general conclusions could be drawn.

There had already been considerable discussion about these difficulties and their causes in the secondary school. Disaffection from the education system resulting from 'coherent attitudinal matrices' based on family or sub-cultural social learning experiences (Rutter *et al.*, 1975; Willis, 1977) or un-successful interactions with a curriculum perceived as irrelevant, were seen as sustaining a cycle of rejection and counter-rejection (Hargreaves *et al.*, 1975; Tattum, 1982). In other cases, maturational retardation or unsatisfactory social learning experiences limited children's ability to relate successfully within the large groups found in mainstream classrooms (Newcomer, 1980; Ross, 1974). It appeared, however, that relatively little evidence was available about the existence of the problems in primary schools. For this reason, together with the growing level of exclusion being reported, it appeared that this was a propitious time to examine emotional and behavioural difficulties in a context where, it was generally agreed by (amongst others) Mortimore *et al.* (1988) that the complicating issues of disaffection and adolescent alienation were largely absent.

Problems of Definition

In order that any phenomenon may be studied, it is essential that a clear view exists as to what it is. The problem is that the concept of emotional and behavioural difficulties (and that of maladjustment which it has replaced), has been dogged by the central difficulty of synthesizing an agreed, coherent, comprehensive and cogent description of the phenomenon from the plethora of accounts and theories advanced. This has led not only to criticism (Laslett, 1983) of 'official' attempts at definition, in particular those in the 1945 regulations (DES, 1945) and the Underwood Report (DES, 1955), but also to some debate as to the nature of the failure to agree. For some, the 'changing perceptions' identified by Laslett (1983) reflect a gradual unfolding of understanding (Davie, 1986; Lund, 1990), while for others (Grace, 1987; Peagam, 1993) they represent merely the current status in the constant struggle for hegemony between rival ideologies. Nor is this ideological struggle of merely academic interest to teachers, since the power of definition carries with it the power to prescribe an appropriate response and thus take control of the resources which are to be applied. Given the degree to which theories of human behaviour are underdetermined by the facts, in that:

> theories may be incompatible with each other and yet compatible with all available data. (Lukes, 1981)

And the extent to which:

> moral and political positions are also at issue in theoretical disputes (*ibid.*, p. 397)

the issue of the locus of definition assumes considerable importance.

One major difficulty is the absence of universal agreement about the nature, origins or even existence of the phenomenon. Instead, a range of competing models has been offered, each rooted in the conceptual framework of the discipline that gave rise to it. As far as professionals within the system are concerned, the four main models (medical, epidemiological, behavioural and interactionist) have been well documented (Laslett, 1983; Davie, 1989), but this is not the sum total of difficulties in definition, since teachers do not entirely inhabit a universe where such 'professional' understandings hold sway. Education takes place within a public and political arena, and the conceptual models which inform the debate also impinge upon teacher understanding of the nature of, and appropriate response to children's difficulties. This provides two other important models to be taken into account.

The 'Original Sin' model, (very dear to 'the man on the Clapham Omnibus') based on 'common-sense' understandings of the inherently perverse nature of the human species and the voluntary nature of deviance has a long tradition in the interpretation of deviant behaviour. From the notion of the 'sins of Adam' that each child inherits (Allestree, 1658) through the need to 'break the will' (Wesley, 1872) and the 'mental hygienist' approaches of (Liddiard, 1928) to the requirement to 'place the responsibility for the child's behaviour firmly where it should be placed: on the child' (Meek, 1986), there is a concern to ensure that individual responsibility is recognized, so that the then Secretary of State felt able to observe in an article in *The Spectator* (7 April 1992):

it is self-evident that individuals choose whether to be good or bad.

Meanwhile, for parents, the 'discounting' theory of personality described by Mills and Rubin (1990) with its acceptance of 'that's just the way he is' as an adequate explanation dismisses the causal explanations offered by professionals and renders further investigation unnecessary.

At the other extreme, the 'societal' model, which examines the role of social formations in the creation and definition of disturbance (Bowman, 1981) has been interpreted through a number of traditions. Pluralist and Neo-pluralist (Grace, 1987; Elton, 1989); Marxist (Althusser, 1972; Lawn and Ozga, 1988); and Neo-Marxist (Riseborough, 1985) models have all been employed to explain deteriorating relationships in schools. Others (Willis, 1977; Simon, 1980) have identified the potential for conflict inherent in the transmission of an alien culture in schools where children are already steeped in their own working class counter-culture.

Given this range of models, it is easy to agree with Shears (1978) that:

In fact there are enough theories so that one may be chosen to suit any personal prejudice and any conception. (p. 57)

Moreover, there is often not even agreement among commentators as to which model is actually in evidence. While Lund (1990) asserted that the medical model has faded, and that the Elton Report strengthened current alternative trends, Upton and Cooper (1990), saw in that same report evidence that the Committee chose for its

> assumptions about the nature of the problem those of the medical model. (p. 7)

The confusion in and around the Elton Report (see Peagam and Upton, 1991) that what an individual observes is a function of his own theories and expectations, as much as of any inherent reality in the phenomenon being observed serves to indicate the difficulties encountered in seeking a 'factual' basis for understanding emotional and behavioural difficulties.

Attempts to integrate these models and the understandings they support into a coherent eclectic approach have been thwarted by the inherent difficulty of negotiation between paradigms based on different conceptual frameworks and underpinned by different value and belief systems (Habermas, 1972). Thus, not only do they compete, but those success indicators that persuade adherents of the validity of their chosen model, may be rejected as worthless or irrelevant by proponents of other models. This has led to a series of (often rancorous) debates both within and across professional groups about appropriate responses to 'difficult' behaviour, and the limits to 'treatment'. At an educational level, the debate has sometimes been equally acrimonious as evidenced by the angry response from psychologists to the treatment of behavioural approaches in Open University course material (Swann, 1982).

For teachers, some of the difficulties arise from the fact that school-based responses to emotional/behavioural difficulties have been driven by taxonomies of disturbance developed within other disciplines (for example, psychiatrists, psychologists, psychotherapists, social workers), and have, particularly since the 1981 Education Act, been operated against the background of what is now coming to be more widely recognized as the mistaken view that 'emotional and behavioural difficulties' can be equated with physical, cognitive, or sensory handicaps for the purpose of determining appropriate educational provision.

The fact that issues of definition, diagnosis and prescription have tended to be seen as the province of these outside professionals, has caused considerable confusion about the role and status of teachers. This is less problematic with physical or sensory handicap where the professional roles are more clearly differentiated, but the lack of clear boundaries in this area, creates a potential for significant angst arising from perceived professional encroachment (Tomlinson, 1982). This difficulty is exacerbated by the absence of any nationally validated, inter-professionally recognized qualification for teaching children with emotional and behavioural difficulties. The availability and requirement to obtain such a qualification for teachers of children with vision or hearing difficulties, not only provides evidence of competence and therefore status, but, being based on a body of theory and knowledge, establishes that theory and knowledge as the recognized basis for expertise. Teachers, deprived of the power to define the task boundaries relating to behaviour through 'special educational need' expertise are, consequently driven to use exclusion as an alternative structure for definition.

Developing an Appropriate Model

Where conflicting interpretations result from conceptual pluralism, any practical response requires this conflict to be resolved, or at least managed, to establish a set of working definitions, which can then be evaluated in terms of the prescribed model. One valid approach is via a 'contingency' model (Tyler, 1988), where a flexible, context-dependent approach to definition and reference group is adopted. In this case the aim was to establish a view as to the prevalence, extent and distribution of difficulties. In the sense that politics is the development of a response to conflicting views and/or interests, the issue of what is, or is not to be perceived as disturbed behaviour is essentially a political one, since it rests on the definition of the boundaries to the teacher's task. Emotional and behavioural difficulties, it has been argued, (Galloway, 1985), must be seen as not only context dependent, but also incapable of being classified according to objective norms, since maladaptive behaviour is inevitably defined according to the norms of others. Moreover, when a child inhabits regions with conflicting norms, the degree to which social institutions, and particularly schools, are, or should be, free to accommodate behaviour which conflicts with institutional norms, is, in this sense, a political issue. From this standpoint the question in dispute is not the nature of the behaviour, but the selection of a reference group by whose norms 'disturbed' behaviour is to be defined. For the purpose of this study, therefore, teachers were consciously selected as the primary reference group and any model therefore was required to be relevant to their experience and perceptions.

Interviews with Teachers and Other Professionals

The first stage of the research was an examination through extended interviews of the views of a range of teachers and other education workers on the extent and nature of difficulties which children presented or exhibited, and the adequacy of the various explanations. Thirty-two individuals from a large urban LEA were interviewed during the summer and autumn of 1990. This included twenty-one teachers and headteachers from mainstream and special schools. Among these were a number of class teachers who had been engaged in a 'practice-sharing' project on the management of children's behavioural needs, and were therefore aware of current curriculum and class-management based models. In addition, the views of other professionals were collated to test for radical differences in perception. These comprised medical practitioners (including child psychiatrists) (four), educational psychologists (three), social workers (three) and an education officer with responsibility for statements.

Teachers have traditionally tended to prefer explanations of disturbance which involve some level of pathology, whether the aetiology is seen in terms of emotional disturbance, behaviour disorder, or a reaction to home or environmental deficiencies. This is not to deny that many teachers are aware of alternative explanations and allow for personality and expectation differences as a potential source of conflict. However the interviews replicated the findings of Croll and Moses (1985) where 'within-child' or 'home-based' explanations were identified in over 80 per cent of cases, as opposed to less than 3 per cent for 'in-school' factors. For the teachers interviewed for this study, home and pre-school experiences were still the major determinants of difficult and disturbed behaviour, and suggestions that such difficulties could be largely eliminated by behavioural approaches, and the deployment of appropriate classroom management skills was firmly rejected. While they accepted that schools could, by inappropriate or insensitive handling of children, promote or exacerbate deviant responses, in the main, difficulties were seen to arrive in school with the child, and the school was expected to ameliorate the difficulties to limit the degree to which these constituted a barrier to learning.

This view was supported regardless of the individual teacher's age or length of experience. It therefore appears that, in spite of arguments advanced for other models, teachers in primary schools prefer this model, and this is not through ignorance. Nor does it seem to be purely heuristic. It is more probably sustained through reflecting the teachers' ideological orientation (Hartley, 1985), their perception of the teacher role which contributed to their decision to become one, to 'pursue humanitarian ideals' (Nias, 1985) and subsequently to protect their investment in what Lortie (1975) characterizes as 'craft pride'. Above all, it defines the role of the teacher in terms of guide, counsellor, and mentor, whose achievements are constrained by the degree to which the child requires remedial support whether in terms of cognitive functioning, or the reorientation of the 'map' on which, 'each child plots experiences in an attempt to make sense of his world' (Wall, 1973).

The persistence of this perception across time, in spite of the impact of competing ideologies, is perhaps not difficult to understand. Recent legislation (especially the 1988 and 1993 Education Acts) and official reports which influence the professional and contractual expectations laid on teachers have emphasized the responsibility of teachers and schools to develop the skills, knowledge and understanding of all children. This has strengthened the complementary expectation that children will arrive at school in an appropriate state for this to be possible, since anything which inhibits that function will be seen as a problem, and, consequently, evidence of 'disturbance' particularly when arising from emotional, behavioural or attitudinal obstacles to individual development. In adopting this stance, teachers were reflecting the position of Thomson and Trippe (1971):

> . . . an emotionally disturbed child from the point of view of the schools, is a child whose needs cannot be met through the *ordinary* provision of elementary and secondary education because of disorders of

behaviour, or disorders of learning, even though the ordinary provisions are *maximally flexible* and orientated towards individualised instruction. (p. 65)

Of course, even this is not straightforward since the definition of 'ordinary provision' is in turn a politically contentious issue. However, accepting this reservation, what remains to be answered, through research is the degree to which home, environmental and pre-school factors can and do significantly diminish the ability of children to relate to the 'ordinary' structures. If there is evidence of a significant level of 'predisposition' (Charlton and George, 1989), then teachers are entitled to a recognition that the response to the issue of emotional and behavioural difficulties is not simply one of professional competence. What is required is an acknowledgement of the dilemma posed for teachers by such difficulties in an education system which, increasingly, not only undervalues social outcomes from successful interventions, but actually forces schools into 'deviance-provocative' modes by overt concentration on predominantly academic attainment targets.

There were, predictably, some differences of emphasis between different professional groups, but overall there was a remarkable level of agreement that, however these difficulties might be described, in general, they were not school generated, but arose from factors within the child's experience or background, so that, while teachers could have an important role in mitigating the effects of such difficulties, the origins lay outside their control, and, more importantly outside their professional expertise. There was, in general, strong support for an overall model of aetiology based on social deficit interpretations, but these were often seen in terms of the effect of macro-social processes impinging on the individual and therefore reflected a societal model. There was clear agreement from all three groups of professionals that there existed a group of children displaying emotional and/or behavioural difficulties, for whom solutions within the current framework of school structures were not possible. In addition, it appeared that there was a group of children who were vulnerable to school processes, and that this vulnerability in turn was located in experiences or processes outside the school. While there was scope for disagreement in identification and 'treatment' approaches, and about the extent or nature of appropriate provision, there was general consent that this was a valid area for research, and that there was sufficient agreement for the development of an appropriate 'contingency' model.

This investigation therefore, took as a starting point, the perception that, when all within-school factors have been eliminated, there remains a group of children who bring to school distress and/or disturbance rooted in their previous or ongoing experiences which has a disabling effect beyond the remediable reach of classroom or curriculum structures, and it is this group that teachers have previously come to regard as 'maladjusted'. It was therefore decided to survey all the primary schools in the LEA to examine the extent of teachers' concerns.

The Survey of Schools

Data was collected by means of questionnaires distributed to all primary schools in the spring of 1991, which invited teachers to provide detailed information in relation to each child who was seen as having or presenting difficulties. This involved a significant time commitment, which, given the other pressures on teacher time could be expected to discourage casual overreporting. Since, in addition, this was not an LEA instigated survey and there were no resource implications, there are strong grounds for believing that the numbers were significantly underreported, and subsequent discussions with headteachers confirmed this. Some form of response was received from over two-thirds of the schools, only one of which suggested that the exercise was invalid. A number of headteachers indicated their support for the project but felt that their schools were too hard-pressed to participate in it. Careful comparisons were made to ensure that the sample was representative.

Teachers were invited to categorize each child they identified as having difficulties in terms of one of six types of problem roughly corresponding to those used in the Underwood Report, and one of five levels of appropriate provision ranging from 'no special arrangements' to 'requires special school or unit'. In addition, teachers were asked to report on a range of issues relating to the child's background, performance and relationships within the school, and home-school cooperation. The information was then examined, both for common factors in the children identified, and differences between the children whom teachers identified given a free choice, and those who emerged with statements.

In all 874 questionnaires (each one providing information on one child) were returned from 176 schools, corresponding to approximately 2 per cent of the total child population of those schools. Even allowing for the reasons for underreporting already discussed, this was lower than might have been expected, given that for similar populations researchers with psychiatric backgrounds (for example, Richman *et al.*, 1982; Newth and Corbett, 1993) have consistently recorded from 4–7 per cent of children as having serious emotional disturbance. Nor did this match up with the consistent opinions expressed by teachers during the survey that the situation was deteriorating, especially since when the same population was surveyed for the Underwood Report (DES, 1955), some 15 per cent were found to be 'probably maladjusted' with 0.6 per cent 'very maladjusted, needing special treatment by a child guidance team'. The explanation for the fact that the size of this latter group had remained fairly constant while the 'probables' had declined may have been the degree to which teachers had accepted alternative strategies and embraced 'whole-school' approaches to behaviour management. This would suggest that the 'very maladjusted' category of Underwood corresponded to those who required outside intervention, (approximately 0.6 per cent of the total population) with a marked decline (to 1.2 per cent) in the numbers seen as having difficulties of a lesser order.

Subsequent investigations in responding schools indicated that as a result of altered structures and perceptions, many children who would once have been identified as being 'maladjusted', had been helped to succeed, while for others, expectations about pupil attitudes and task orientation had altered or (as some would argue) declined. Consequently, teachers were identifying a smaller, but more troublesome group of children who presented difficulties beyond the scope of behaviour policies, and whose response frustrated the operation of those very policies. Nevertheless, the fact that teachers still felt that, given adequate support, less than 0.1 per cent of their pupils required segregated provision, clearly indicated their acceptance of the principle of integration.

Perhaps not surprisingly 'conduct' (or externalized) difficulties predominated, for nearly two-thirds of those identified, with 'nervous' or internalized difficulties making up a further quarter. This showed a shift in the proportions reported by Rutter (1975) and Croll and Moses (1985), and perhaps reflected a growing concern about disruption in the face of increasing demands for teachers to achieve according to externally determined 'performance indicators'. What was less predictable was the consistency of recorded concerns across the whole age group. Thus the difficulties were seen as evenly distributed throughout the years, rather than concentrated at the upper end.

It is not possible here to document the detailed findings of the research report (Peagam, 1993), but it is worth commenting on some interesting patterns that emerged. It was clear from a comparison of the backgrounds of the children identified with those of the population as a whole that the predominant 'person specification' was that of a male child of an unskilled or unemployed manual worker, living with a single parent or in a reconstituted family, in council housing with an income sufficiently low to entitle him to free dinners. There was thus clear evidence of a socioeconomic bias either in terms of the development of difficulties, or in the identification of them among what many observers are coming to see as an 'underclass'. In this respect, as in terms of the overrepresentation of Afro-Caribbean children (Peagam, 1994), the children identified reflected the population of the LEA's 'EBD' provision, while areas where schools reported greatest numbers were also, in the main, those which contributed most pupils to that provision. What was also interesting was that such schools were not exclusively or even generally found in 'inner-city' areas. What they did have in common, generally, was location on run-down municipal estates, with high levels of pupil mobility, and low levels of community identity. Nor were these schools all obviously failing, and, in fact, many had adapted their approach to accommodate what they saw as their distinctive role, developing group and individual strategies to enable children to succeed, where a more orthodox approach might well have resulted in wholesale exclusions. What did cause considerable anxiety was the prospect of inspection according to a framework which took little account of their special problems and achievements. There was also a real concern that a reputation for coping with the needs of these children would not only attract more problems, but also might encourage parents whose children did not have such problems to opt for another school.

Summary and Conclusions

This survey replicates the conclusions of other surveys of teacher attitudes, particularly Shears (1978) and Croll and Moses (1985) confirming teacher belief that, whatever may be argued elsewhere, these difficulties do, in fact, exist, they arrive in school with the child, and they are almost entirely the result of previous or continuing experiences in the children's background. Croll and Moses (1985) saw this as resulting from teacher familiarity with child and home-based explanations, and their unfamiliarity with alternatives. Whether or not this argument was valid in 1985, it is hard to believe that teachers were still in ignorance of such alternative explanations in 1990, given the orientation of the Elton Report (Elton, 1989), and the publicity which has surrounded school effectiveness studies, especially Rutter *et al.* (1979) and Rutter (1983). More-over the evidence from the interviews strongly suggested that teachers have in fact considered and rejected other models.

At the same time attempts by educational psychologists to introduce be-havioural approaches to difficult children in many schools appear to have foundered, as much because of teacher rejection of the philosophical impli-cations as because of their perceived impracticality. Meanwhile, pressures on teachers to adopt different work practices and attitudes, not only to comply with the National Curriculum, but also to ensure the 'marketability' of the school appear to be lessening the confidence of some schools in their ability to accommodate the children who cannot embrace these practices and attitudes.

Teachers therefore prefer a model within which pedagogic and counsel-ling skills ameliorate the effects of damage done elsewhere. However, what-ever the origins, some children's emotional difficulties and behaviour problems are seen as transcending classroom structures and teacher skills, given the primary task of provision of satisfactory educational experiences to the whole group. Not only is this constrained by teachers' perceptions, the increase in parental influence especially since the 1986 Act has created pressure to avoid being seen to devote disproportionate time and energy to such children, while the likelihood of parental criticism that other children's chances are affected by their behaviour, can reduce tolerance towards difficult children. One conse-quence has been the ever-increasing spiral of children offered for 'statementing', or, where this route is blocked, a steady rise in exclusions from school.

For the majority, however, there is agreement that the response should be developed within the mainstream of educational provision. The evidence of both the interviews and the questionnaires in this survey shows that the great majority of primary school behaviour problems are seen as 'containable' with support within the mainstream. The point at issue is the cost in emotional terms to the teacher and the other pupils, and the learning opportunity cost to the whole class. It is this emotional impact on the teacher that is obfuscated by mechanistic approaches such as that of Gray and Ruddock whose research for the Elton Committee merely sought to quantify specific behaviours. It was clear from this survey that the unpredictable nature of many childrens' responses caused concern to teachers, and they pointed to the resultant anxiety and uncertainty with consequent increase in stress levels. Approaches to the problem therefore would need to address two objectives; to reduce the perceived cost to a point where it was seen as sustainable, and to enable teachers to feel good about any increased level of commitment required. It would also be necessary to reassure teachers that 'containment' at primary school level is not simply postponement of breakdown until the child reaches the secondary school. The process must be believed to be actually having a positive effect on the child if teachers are to feel the effort is justified.

What seems clear, and in tune with the educational approach of many primary school teachers, is the need for a creative response which validates the perceptions and expertise of teachers. If they feel imposed upon, as many appear to, not only by curriculum requirements, but also the need to cope with what they see as increasingly alienated pupil attitudes, while being publicly pilloried for alleged falling reading standards, there will be a pressure to unload some of the burden. The effects of the 1988 and 1993 Acts is likely to be a continued increase in concerns about behaviour problems, and a diminution of the LEA's power to intervene to address them. Meanwhile, the structured valuation of academic as opposed to social outcomes will encourage schools to see exclusion as the appropriate response to serious behaviour problems and, given that government policies, effectively encourage this approach, ministerial interventions to reduce the use of exclusion are likely to fail. Positive strategies can still be developed, but this will require a fundamental shift in the values of government and others if schools and LEA's are to be encouraged to pursue them. It is important that specialist expertise in this area should be genuinely valued and accredited, with attachment to special education or support services seen as an important stage in career development for highly competent class teachers rather than 'career death'. Otherwise there is a real risk that increasing numbers of children from this 'underclass' will end up being taught by a new teacher underclass.

References

ALLESTREE, R. (1658) *The Whole Duty of Man*, London.
ALTHUSSER, L. (1972) 'Ideology and ideological state apparatus', in COSIN, B.R. (Ed) *Education: Structure and Society*, Harmondsworth, Penguin Books.
BOWMAN, I. (1981) 'Maladjustment: A history of the category', In SWANN, W. (Ed) *The Practice of Special Education*, Oxford, Blackwell.
CHALMERS, A. (1976) *What is this Thing called Science?*, Queensland, University of Queensland.

CHARLTON, T. and GEORGE, J. (1989) 'The development of behaviour problems', in CHARLTON, T. and DAVID, K. (Eds) *Managing Misbehaviour*, Basingstoke, Macmillan Educational.

CROLL, P and MOSES, D. (1985) *One in Five: The Assessment and Incidence of Special Educational Needs*, London, Routledge and Kegan Paul.

DAVIE, R. (1986) 'Understanding behaviour problems', *Maladjustment and Therapeutic Education*, **4**, 1, pp. 2–11.

DAVIE, R. (1989) 'Behaviour problems and the teacher', in CHARLTON T. and DAVID, K. (Eds) *Managing Misbehaviour*, Basingstoke, Macmillan Education.

DES (1945) *The Handicapped Persons and School Health Regulations*, London, HMSO.

DES (1955) *Report of the Committee on Maladjusted Children. (The Underwood Report)*, London, HMSO.

ELTON, LORD (1989) *Discipline in Schools: A Report of the Committee of Enquiry*, London, HMSO.

GALLOWAY, D. (1985) *Schools, Pupils and Special Educational Needs*, London, Croom Helm.

GRACE, G. (1987) 'Teachers and the state in Britain', in LAWN, M. and GRACE, G. (Eds) *Teachers: The Culture and Politics of Work*, Lewes, Falmer Press.

HABERMAS, J. (1972) *Knowledge and Human Interests. (Trans.)*, London, Heinemann.

HARGREAVES, D., HESTOR, S. and MELLOR, F. (1975) *Deviance in Classrooms*, London, Routledge and Kegan Paul.

HARTLEY, D. (1985) *Understanding the Primary School*, London, Croom Helm.

LASLETT, R. (1983) *Changing Perceptions of Maladjusted Children*, Portishead, AWMC.

LAWN, M. and OZGA, J. (1988) 'The educational worker? A reassessment of teachers', in OZGA, J. (Ed) *Schoolwork: Approaches to the Labour Process of Teaching*, Milton Keynes, Open University Press.

LIDDIARD, M. (1928) *The Mothercraft Manual*, London, Churchill.

LORTIE, D. (1975) *Schoolteacher: A Sociological Study*, Chicago, IL, University of Chicago Press.

LUKES, S. (1981) 'Fact and theory in the social sciences', in POTTER, D. (Ed) *Society and the Social Sciences: An Introduction*, London, Routledge and Kegan Paul.

LUND, R. (1990) 'Curriculum development for children with emotional and behavioural difficulties and the introduction of the National Curriculum', *Maladjustment and Therapeutic Education*, **8**, 2, pp. 74–82.

MEEK, P.J. (1986) 'Standards of behaviour: A new approach', *Education Today: Journal of the College of Preceptors*, **36**, 3, pp. 51–7.

MILLS, R.S.L. and RUBIN, K.H. (1990) 'Parental beliefs about problematic social behaviours in childhood', *Child Development*, **61**, 1, pp. 138–51.

MORTIMORE, P., SAMMONS, P., STOLL, L., LEWIS, D. and ECOB, R. (1988) *School Matters: The Junior Years*, Wells, Open Books.

NEWCOMER, P.L. (1980) *Understanding and Teaching Emotionally Disturbed Children*, Boston, Allyn and Bacon.

NEWTH, S. and CORBETT, J. (1993) 'Behaviour and emotional problems in 3-year-old children of Asian parentage', *Journal of Child Psychology and Psychiatry*, **34**, 3, pp. 333–52.

NIAS, J. (1985) 'What it means to feel like a teacher: The subjective reality of primary school teaching', in OZGA, J. (Ed) *Schoolwork: Approaches to the Labour Process of Teaching*, Milton Keynes, Open University Press.

PEAGAM, E. (1993) '*The incidence and nature of emotional and behavioural difficulties in the primary school population of a Midlands LEA*', unpublished PhD thesis, University of Birmingham.

PEAGAM, E. (1994) 'Special needs or educational apartheid? The emotional and behavioural difficulties of Afro-Caribbean children', *Support for Learning*, **9**, 1, pp. 33–9.

PEAGAM, E. and UPTON, G. (1991) 'Emotional and behavioural difficulties and the Elton Report', *Maladjustment and Therapeutic Education*, **9**, 1, pp. 41–8.

RICHMAN, N., STEVENSON, J. and GRAHAM, P.J. (1982) *Pre-School to School: A Behavioural Study*, London, Academic Press.

RISEBOROUGH, G. (1985) 'Pupils, teachers' careers and schooling: An empirical study', in BALL, S. and GOODSON, I. (Eds) *Teachers' Lives and Careers*, Lewes, Falmer Press.

ROSS, A.O. (1974) *Psychological Disorders of Children*, New York, McGraw Hill.

RUTTER, M. (1975) *Helping Troubled Children*, Harmondsworth, Penguin.

RUTTER, M. (1983) 'School effects on pupil progress — findings and policy implications', *Child Development*, **54**, 1, pp. 1–29.

RUTTER, M., COX, A., TUPLING, C., BERGER, M. and YULE, W. (1975) 'Attainment and adjustment in two geographical areas: The prevalence of psychiatric disorder', *British Journal of Psychiatry*, **126**, pp. 493–509.

RUTTER, M., MAUGHAN, B. MORTIMORE, P. and OUSTON, J. (1979) *Fifteen Thousand Hours: Secondary Schools and Their Effects on Children*, London, Open Books.

SHEARS, B. (1978) *'Teachers' concepts of maladjustment'*, Unpublished MEd thesis, University of Birmingham.

SIMON, B. (1980) 'Problems in contemporary educational theory: A Marxist approach', in FINCH, A. and SCRIMSHAW, P. (Eds) *Standards, Schooling and Education*, Sevenoaks, Hodder and Stoughton.

SWANN, W. (1982) *Special Needs in Education, Unit 12: Psychology and Special Education*, Milton Keynes, Open University Press.

TATTUM, D.P. (1982) *Disruptive Pupils in Schools and Units*, Chichester, Wiley.

THOMSON, A.C. and TRIPPE, J.J. (1971) 'A school-based definition of emotionally disturbed children', in CRUIKSHANK, W. (Ed) *Psychology of Exceptional Children and Youth*, Boston, MA, Allyn and Bacon.

TOMLINSON, S. (1982) *A Sociology of Special Education*, London, Routledge and Kegan Paul.

TYLER, W. (1988) *School Organisation: A Sociological Perspective*, London, Croom Helm.

UPTON, G. and COOPER, P. (1990) 'A new perspective on behaviour problems in schools: The ecosystemic approach', *Maladjustment and Therapeutic Education*, **8**, 1, pp. 3–18.

WALL, W. (1973) 'The problem child in schools', in WALL, W. (Ed) *The Problem Child and The Psychological Services*, London, Education Review.

WESLEY, J. (1872) *Works*, London, Wesleyan Conference Office.

WILLIS, P. (1977) *Learning to Labour*, London, Saxon House.

Chapter 4

Emotional Abuse: Identification and Assessment in an Education Setting

Pauline Collier

Rejection, isolation, humiliation, verbal assaults, being ignored, being terrorised — these are things that happen to children. These are the things that crush a child's self-esteem, taint a child's emotional well-being and damage a child's potential to contribute fully in this world. (Brassard, Germain and Hart, 1987)

Introduction

Throughout my educational history, quotations have always held a very special place for me. Some quotations seem to have the magic to capture the essence of a situation or idea in a very simple but very powerful way. This quotation from the foreword to *The Psychological Maltreatment of Children and Youth* by Brassard, Germain and Hart captures for me the essence of emotional abuse. My aim in this chapter is to consider and analyze these words in greater detail. The questions I shall be looking at are:

(i)   What is emotional abuse?
(ii)   What is emotionally abusive parenting?
(iii) What are the consequences for children and young people?
(iv)   How can it be assessed?
(v)   What is the role of education staff in this process?

My starting point is that education staff, including workers with the under 5s, are the main witnesses to the behavioural signs and indicators which suggest that a child may be being harmed by emotionally abusive parenting. These are the children and young people who probably cause the greatest concern to teachers; these are the children who, because of their emotional and behavioural difficulties, are referred in great numbers to educational psychologists and these are the children who are most demanding in terms of extra time, attention and patience. I am well aware that being in education at the moment is a little bit like being stuck in the middle of a bad dream with each new week bringing new crises, new regulations, new impositions, but child protection is not a new imposition. Education staff have always been concerned about the health and safety of the children and young people in their care. The crucial role of teachers in this area was recognized as long ago as 1973 when the death of Maria Colwell at the age of 7 years brought it home to everyone that children are not just ill-treated by their families, they are sometimes killed by them. The report of the inquiry which looked into the circumstances surrounding her death stated: 'Of all the caring agencies involved with the Colwell family it was her teacher Mrs. Turner, who picked up Maria and noticed how light and thin she was. It was the teacher in whom Maria felt able to confide' (The Maria Colwell Report, 1974). Unfortunately, in those days there were no procedures for schools to follow and vital information was not shared with other key agencies. Of course the situation is different now. Under the Children Act 1989, education staff, if they have knowledge or a suspicion that a child is suffering significant harm have a duty to refer their concern to the Social Services Department or the Police.

What is Emotional Abuse?

In August 1980 the DHSS circulated a memorandum recommending that emotional abuse should be included as a category for placing a child's name on the Child Protection Register. The intervening years have seen little professional intervention under this category of child abuse compared with other types of abuse. This probably reflects less the true incidence of emotional harm than the very significant difficulties in implementing the concept in a child protection context.

Incidence of Emotional Abuse

The low reported incidence of emotional abuse is clearly illustrated in the NSPCC Register Research compiled for the three-year period January 1988 to December 1990. During this period the names of 9628 children were placed on the Child Protection Registers. Of those, 240 (2 per cent) were registered under the category of emotional abuse. In my view, the figure of 2 per cent nowhere near tells the story of the incidence of emotional abuse and many other factors need to be taken into consideration. Professionals realize that emotional abuse is widespread yet Child Protection Registers seldom record it. One of the reasons for this lies in the fact that physical and sexual abuse have been heavily sensationalized by the media because by their very nature they are crisis-laden. Emotional abuse is a chronic condition. The suffering is slow, proceeding over weeks, months and years. Consequently, social workers and their managers remain preoccupied with the physical and sexual aspects of abuse and government guidelines continue to recommend that child protection registers artificially list children in discrete categories. In case conferences, discussion on the emotional and psychological aspects of a child's life is only a fraction of the discussion time spent on 'hard' physical evidence. However, an account of a child's social, emotional and educational life can be far more revealing.

Emotional Abuse as the Core Issue

Research, expert opinion and professional experience agree that emotional and psychological abuse are at the core of all forms of child abuse;

> While emotional maltreatment may occur alone, it often accompanies physical abuse and sexual abuse. Emotionally maltreated children are not always physically abused but physically abused children are almost always emotionally maltreated as well. (Lauer *et al.*, 1979)

Physical abuse and sexual abuse are different ways of harming a child's emotions. The fracture or bruises may be well healed but the feelings and emotions accompanying the injury may take much longer to get better and sometimes never do. Not only does emotional abuse cause developmental harm to children, it can cause long term emotional distress in adults (Brassard *et al.*, 1987). The position of emotional abuse at the core of all child abuse is not only a matter of theoretical interest. It has implications for child care practice in terms of how information is collected, the status of different types of information and the hypotheses that are generated as a result. Kieran O'Hagan, writing in his recent book *Emotional and Psychological Abuse of Children* supports this point:

> In its emphasis on 'emotional' and 'mental' (i.e. psychological) development, the Act will compel practitioners, trainers, managers, solicitors and magistrates to widen their perspective on child abuse generally and to learn how to cope with emotional and psychological abuse in particular. (O'Hagan, 1993)

The bulk of the information on the child's emotional and psychological health is brought to the child protection jigsaw puzzle by education staff. It is important, therefore, that the status and quality of this information is increased, not only at case conferences but in the eyes of the judiciary.

Definitions and Difficulties

The damage done to the psychological and emotional health of children by emotionally abusive parenting has long been recognized by professionals working with children. However, there has never been a clear professional agreement as to what constitutes emotional abuse. For example, at what point does a 'shouting' parent become a 'terrorizing' parent and at what point does 'criticism' become 'humiliation'?

Some researchers have looked to the characteristics of parents for explanations of emotionally abusive parenting. They have identified mental illness, alcohol and drug dependency, marital conflict, and the parents own impoverished childhoods as predisposing factors. They have identified parents who are lacking in attachment, lacking in commitment, those who are disinterested and those who always prioritize their own interests first. They have identified those who have seriously unrealistic expectations of their children and those who see their children as 'lacking in cooperation'.

Other workers have concentrated on the social and economic circumstances surrounding emotionally unhealthy families. Families who are isolated and rejected by the community. Families where poverty, crime and poor housing 'label' them as worthless. Families where there is a culture of 'distrust or rejection' of the outside world or have lifestyles (for example, nomadic or drug using) which perpetually destroy the potential for friendships and support systems to develop and finally where parents have no experiences of good parenting and are ignorant of the child's needs and capabilities. It is not surprising that in these circumstances, parental coping skills are overwhelmed.

All professionals are familiar with those families where all the members, both adults and children are victims in some way and where their very life circumstances are abusive. However, there are also parents who live in the most privileged circumstances who remain psychologically unfit to meet the emotional needs of their children. Whatever the family circumstances, the Children Act 1989 clearly states that the welfare of the child is paramount and that parents now have a legal responsibility to meet the physical, intellectual, emotional and social needs of their children.

So far we have looked at the characteristics of parents and we have also considered the socioeconomic factors which affect parenting. In addition some workers feel that children themselves have features which elicit abusive parenting. Children who as babies cry a lot and sleep little. Children who are overactive as well as children who seem placid and docile, boys who resemble their fathers and become the scapegoat of mothers too frightened to confront the real perpetrator of their distress. In fact the interaction between poor parenting and children's behaviours in terms of which came first is always difficult to disentangle.

Emotional Abuse in Education

Parents of course are not the only ones who abuse children. Because of their relatively powerless position in society, they are vulnerable to all adults. The Open University Pack on Child Abuse and Neglect (1989) contains a number of case studies, one of which is as follows:

Miss Winter is Lee's teacher. Lee is 8 and disruptive and difficult, and has behaviour problems, like wetting his pants. In a moment of frustration when he has been particularly naughty, Miss Winter called him a '. . . dirty stinking boy' in front of the whole class and made him wear a pair of girl's pink shorts as a punishment.

We are all capable of harsh, cruel words in a moment of tiredness and frustration but equally I'm sure we are all familiar with teachers who control children through sarcasm and humiliation — and are proud of it! There are in fact teachers who display the same behavioural characteristics as those parents who emotionally ill-treat children. Schools are not always emotionally healthy places in which to be.

Emotional Abuse in Social Work

Jones and Novak (1991) observe that British social work journals report virtually every week on some accusation or conviction of individuals for offenses against children entrusted to their care. We have seen the case of Frank Beck who over a period of many years was responsible for physically, sexually, and emotionally abusing children in his care. The inquiry report into the use of 'Pin-down' in a number of Staffordshire children's homes and family centres contains abundant examples of emotional and psychological abuse of children by staff.

Emotional Abuse in the Playground

In our own schools at playtimes we see the fear and unhappiness in children who are being bullied by their peers. Bullying might be racist, sexist, or because a child is too fat or too thin, or too clever or not clever enough, or because a young person is developing a sexual orientation which is not heterosexual. Such behaviour between children and young people is not 'just a joke Miss' nor is it 'character building'. It is emotionally hurtful and psychologically destructive; it can lead to truancy and in some cases has led to the suicide of the young person involved. The saying 'Sticks and stones may break my bones but names will never hurt me' is plainly untrue.

Children's Rights

This chapter though is not about all aspects of emotional abuse. Its focus is on emotionally abusive parenting within the context of our child protection procedures as defined by *Working Together Under the Children Act 1989*. The framework I have found useful in looking at emotionally abusive parenting has the concept of Children's Rights as its starting point.

In order to mark the occasion of 1979 the International Year of the Child the International School Psychology Association produced a document called the *Declaration of the Psychological Rights of the Child.* Ten years later, in 1989, the United Nations Convention on the Rights of Children was signed by ninety nations although this did not include Britain. This country has not articulated nor committed itself to a positive ideology of children which values them in their own right. This was summarized by the Children's Legal Centre in its response to the publication of the Cleveland Inquiry Report which it saw as a milestone in the development of children's rights to be treated as people and not simply as objects of concern:

> In our view the major cause of all kinds of abuse of children in our society — physical, emotional, and sexual arises from deeply rooted and negative attitudes to children. Until children are recognised as individual people with rights of their own, including developing rights to self-determination and equal rights to legal protection from all kinds of assault, they will continue to be dominated, degraded and abused, and frequently will feel powerless to complain or stop the abuse. (Children's Legal Centre, 1988)

In spite of this, it is worth considering the list of children's rights published by the Royal College of Psychiatrists:

   (i)   Physical care and protection;
   (ii)   Affection and approval;
   (iii)   Stimulation and teaching;
   (iv)   Discipline and control which are consistent and age appropriate;
   (v)   Opportunity and encouragement to gradually acquire autonomy.

To these basic needs the Royal College of Psychiatrists adds the following to ensure a child's good mental health:

   (vi)   Appropriate physical contact;
   (vii)   Emotional support and containment in times of stress;
   (viii)   Recognition of the child as a separate individual.
(Royal College of Psychiatrists, 1982)

The Children Act 1989 stresses that these basic needs of children in our society are best met within the family and in order to consolidate this view, it has as one of its major themes that of parental responsibility. Parent's rights are no longer automatic but rooted in their willingness and ability to carry out their responsibilities. What then does a parent have to do to provide an environment which makes it possible for a child to grow up emotionally and psychologically healthy. Covitz (1986) describes a child's emotional needs as follows:

A child facing the difficult challenge of growing up, needs a number of things from (her/his) parents: their backing and support; their love and encouragement; a sense of stability in the family bond; affectionate exchanges with family members; positive role models and a sense that (her/his) parents love life. A child needs to be liked as a person, a unique individual.

What is Emotionally Abusive Parenting?

There appears to be common agreement amongst professional groups, that emotional abuse is the failure of parents or carers to meet the emotional needs of children and young people. Very few parents though, if any, can meet all the needs of all their children all the time. However, most parents do achieve parenting which does not impede or seriously damage development but the behaviour of some parents towards their children does require intervention. The Children Act 1989 offers this definition of emotional abuse:

> the actual or likely severe adverse effect on the emotional and behavioural development of a child caused by persistent or severe emotional ill-treatment or rejection. All abuse involves some emotional ill-treatment. (Working Together, 1991)

The list of parenting behaviours which experts and professionals generally agree to be emotionally abusive are as follows:

Rejecting — Talking to or talking about a child in a way which suggests dislike. Refusing to help a child or acknowledge their requests for assistance.

Degrading — Labelling a child as inferior, worthless or unlovable. Morbid teasing, constant belittlement, public humiliation.

Terrorizing — Threatening to harm the child, to leave home or leave the child unattended. Allowing a child to witness violence towards loved ones. Alternately indulging and abusing so the child is unable to predict adults' moods and behaviours.

Isolating — Not allowing the child to mix with other children or adults. Locking the child in a cupboard or a room alone for extended periods.

Corrupting — Teaching hate by reinforcing acts that degrade others. Teaching and reinforcing criminal acts. Teaching and reinforcing anti-social behaviour as usual or appropriate for example, aggression

Exploiting — Using the child solely to gratify adult needs, for example,

Pauline Collier

pornography or other sexual practices. Keeping a child at home to act as a servant or a 'parent'.

Denying — Not meeting a child's need for physical affection, praise and encouragement. Not being emotionally available for the child. Denying a child's needs for education, appropriate discipline and appropriate medical attention. (Brassard *et al.*, 1987)

Kieran O'Hagan says that emotional and psychological abuse is perpetrated against children regardless of their age, culture, religion, or class. He also says that:

Numerous categories of parents/carers have been identified as frequent though unwitting and unwilling perpetrators of such abuse. These parents are not horror specimens, unique in pathology or cruelty; they are ordinary people, representative of thousands of parents/ carers, who, as a consequence of their misfortune (over which many of them have no control), cannot avoid emotionally and psychologically abusing their children.

O'Hagan's book is important because unlike most of the American research which uses the term 'psychological maltreatment', he distinguishes between 'emotional' abuse and 'psychological' abuse. First of all, he makes the point that single acts of behaviour do not constitute emotional or psychological abuse. He says that to constitute abuse, the parental behaviour must be repetitive and sustained. It is the abuse that happens everyday, the selfishness, the carelessness and thoughtlessness that damages the quality of a child's emotional life. O'Hagan goes on to say the 'emotion' is about feeling whereas 'the psychological' refers to the mind. He says that there are many emotions, fear, anger, joy, disappointment, love, envy, and despair and the ability to express emotions adequately and appropriately is a crucially important aspect of a child's development. It is easy and common for parents to impede or impair this faculty and, if they do, significant harm is done to the child's emotional development.

On the other hand, 'psychological' development refers to the function and development of mental processes and faculties. He uses the term 'cognition' to cover most of the mental processes and includes intelligence, attention, memory, perception, language, thinking, problem-solving, reasoning, and concept attainment. In addition to these he includes the child's developing moral sense. When any or all of these are impeded or impaired, significant harm is being inflicted on the child's psychological development.

Having made this distinction, however, O'Hagan makes the point that:

. . . emotional and psychological development are closely linked throughout most of one's life, perpetually impinging upon and influencing each other. (O'Hagan, 1993)

What Are the Consequences for Children and Young People?

The current state of knowledge about the consequences to children of emotionally and psychologically abusive parenting comes from a combination of research and expert opinion. This work, most of which has been carried out in North America, is well summarized in Brassard *et al.* (1987). The following list includes most of the outcomes of emotionally abusive parenting:

- Habit disorders, such as sucking, biting, rocking, enuresis or feeding disorders;
- Conduct disorders, including withdrawal and antisocial behaviour such as destructiveness, cruelty and stealing;
- Neurotic traits, such as sleep disorders and inhibition of play;
- Psychoneurotic reactions, including hysteria, obsession, compulsion, phobias and hypochondria;
- Behaviour extremes, such as appearing overly compliant, extremely passive or aggressive, very demanding or undemanding;
- Overly adaptive behaviours which are either inappropriately adult (parenting other children for example) or inappropriately infantile (for example, rocking, headbanging or thumbsucking);
- Lags in emotional and intellectual development;
- Attempted suicide.

Developmental theory suggests that children may be more vulnerable to certain types of negative experience at one developmental stage than another. Garbarino *et al.* (1989) for example, considers the effects of emotionally and psychologically abusive parenting across the period from infancy to adolescence. His view is that infants, children in early childhood, school age children and adolescents respond differently to psychological maltreatment.

Education as Protection

One of the most interesting aspects of work on emotional and psychological abuse is that not all children who have been maltreated by their parents become damaged or go on to become damaged adults (Adcock *et al.*, 1991). O'Hagan says that it is not the parenting per se (rejecting, terrorizing etc) which is abusive but the emotional and psychological impact on the child. In other words, it is the personal subjective meaning for the victim which decides whether or not it is abusive and this is affected by the child's age and stage of development.

Additional factors have also been identified as making a child more or less vulnerable to adverse life circumstances. Rutter (1979) originally identified the concept of 'protective' and 'vulnerability' factors with regard to psychiatric risk. Amongst the factors he felt protected children from being emotionally damaged was a supportive school environment. Emotional and psychological damage, therefore, is not an inevitable outcome of abuse and clearly education staff and schooling, including extra curricular activities, can give protection to children and young people against the most severe consequences of abuse.

Finally in this section I want to raise the dilemma of the difference between emotional abuse and 'growth — inducing challenge' which is illustrated very well by Garbarino *et al.* in their book *The Psychologically Battered Child*:

Strong Words

Have you learned lessons only
from those who admired you
and were tender with you
and stood aside for you?

Have you not learned great lessons
from those who reject you and
brace themselves against you, or
who treat you with contempt, or
dispute the passage with you?
(Garbarino *et al.*, 1989)

The world is not always a friendly, happy place. Both children and adults have to face hardship, loss, criticism, disappointment. Parents and carers sometimes have to judge how much support to give their child. They have to decide when to intervene on their behalf and when not to intervene, when to criticize and when not to criticize. Against a background of affection and support, exposure to the everyday stresses of life can have a beneficial, growth-inducing effect. Without this background though, these everyday stresses can overwhelm a child and maladaptive patterns of behaviour can emerge.

How Can Emotional Abuse be Assessed?

Schools play a particularly important part in protecting children from abuse and a high percentage of child abuse cases are referred by teachers. The importance of this was recognized in DES Circular 4/88, the contents of which were confirmed in *Working Together Under the Children Act* (1989). Further weight has been given to this role by the fact that as part of the new OFSTED inspections. Inspectors will be required to make a judgment about the effectiveness of a school in promoting the welfare, health safety and guidance of its pupils. As part of the evidence for this judgment, inspectors will look at the school's child protection policy and procedures and consider whether they comply with national guidance. As O'Hagan (1993) says:

There is no professional better placed to observe the consequences of psychological abuse than classroom teachers. Work performance, levels of concentration and attentiveness, perception (as manifest through written work, art and play) language and changing relationships within peer groups — all these may be repeatedly observed and monitored over a sufficiently long period to convince teaching staff that there is a serious problem necessitating referral to a child care agency.

How can we raise the status of the information we have as education workers? How can we best present the observations that we have as a result of our daily contact with children? One way would be to follow the conditions laid down in the Children Act 1989 under which a Care Order or Supervision Order may be granted. In my view this would be good practice, even though it might be possible to deal with the case at an earlier stage in the child protection process. Application for a Care Order is not the inevitable outcome of a teacher reporting their concerns.

The Children Act 1989, sets out the conditions for court intervention as follows:

(i) That the child concerned is suffering, or is likely to suffer from SIGNIFICANT HARM and

(ii) That the harm, or likelihood of harm, is attributed to

    (a) the care given to the child, or likely to be given him if the order were not made, not being what it would be reasonable to expect a parent to give him; or

    (b) the child being beyond parental control.

Education staff are not in a position to draw conclusions. We cannot say, even though we may suspect it, that the concerns we have about a child can be attributed to the care given to the child by the parent or carer. Such investigation is the responsibility of the Social Services Department together with any expert witness they may call in to carry out an assessment of the parenting behaviours, the child-located behaviours and the possible causal link between the two.

What we can do is to report any interactions we have seen between the child and their parents. For example, in an interview with a parent about an aspect of their child's school performance, the parent might talk in a way that suggests dislike (rejection) of the child. If this is done in front of the child, the effects may be deeply humiliating. What we are able to give evidence of is the likelihood of significant harm. This is defined as:

Harm — *ill treatment* or the impairment of *health* or *development*;

Ill treatment — this includes sexual abuse and forms of ill treatment which are not physical;

Health — means physical or mental health;

Development — means physical, intellectual, emotional, social and behavioural.

These areas, the intellectual, social, emotional and behavioural aspects of a
child's development are the ones upon which education staff can comment.
These are the areas that educators are trained and qualified to observe. These
are the areas for which schools already have record keeping systems in place.
For child protection work though it is crucial that any records should be
factual, relevant, complete, objective, rumour free, dated and short. A good
test of information contained in child protection records is whether or not it
will withstand any challenge by parents.

One of the crucial issues in determining whether or not a child is being
harmed is whether or not the harm is significant. Eekelaar and Dingwall (1990)
in their book *The Reform of Child Care Law* offer the following comments:

> The Act makes it clear that for harm to be SIGNIFICANT, it must
> be a substantial deficit, with the likelihood of long lasting damage to
> the child, and that it be judged against what might be reasonably
> expected for a similar child. What this means is that the child's devel-
> opment will be charted in accordance with standard developmental
> criteria, such as those prepared for the DHSS by Mary Sheridan.

Unfortunately there is insufficient clarity here for this advice to be really useful. Words such as 'substantial', 'long-lasting' and 'similar child' need further
definition and I suspect that only further research and case law will tease out
these meanings in a way that is really helpful.

What is the Role of Education Staff?

In 1992, Edmundson researched the usefulness of 'emotional abuse' as a concept within an education setting. She discovered that teachers, even designated child protection staff, rarely consider 'emotional abuse' as a cause of
intellectual, emotional and behavioural difficulties in children and do not follow the child protection procedures in such cases. Of the twenty teachers
interviewed who expressed concerns about a child's behaviour and emotional
state, only one had referred the child to the Social Services Department. The
reasons teachers gave for this were:

> the lack of concrete evidence for emotional abuse, the large number
> of children in the class falling into the category, confusion as to the
> nature of emotional abuse, concern about the referral process and not
> regarding the case as serious enough. (Edmundson and Collier, 1993)

The majority of these children were in fact referred to the Educational Psychologist.

Ten years ago the possibility of sexual abuse as an explanation for a child's disturbed emotional state rarely came to mind. Consequently there was little intervention on behalf of these children. Nowadays, sexual abuse is much nearer the top in our list of hypotheses for explaining behavioural disturbance. Perhaps it will only be as a result of research and awareness raising that emotionally abusive parenting will gradually come nearer the top of our list of hypotheses when we seek to explain our concerns about the intellectual, social, emotional and behavioural disturbances of the children and young people in our schools.

The hesitancy of education staff in following child protection procedures on behalf of children who may be being harmed by emotionally abusive parenting may also reflect their very real anxieties about 'making things worse for the child'. Confidence in the child protection process has been badly shaken by media treatment of incidents such as Cleveland (Butler Sloss, 1988) and the Rochdale organized abuse investigations (1990). These both gave rise to images of social workers running off with a child under each arm. It is important to state though that the majority of children on child protection registers remain at home and that only a very small percentage of cases result in care proceedings.

All professionals whose work is concerned with children and families are well placed to recognize signs that a family is under stress and in need of help in the care and parenting of their children. In most cases where concern is expressed, work will be undertaken by the most appropriate agency. Help may come from a range of professionals including Health Visitors, School Nurses, Housing Department staff, Education Department Support Services staff or workers with the under 5s. At this stage, statutory intervention may be unnecessary and inappropriate as the prevention of family breakdown should be a major aim. If, however, the interventions do not reduce or eliminate the concern and child protection procedures are instigated, a case conference is called for the following reasons:

(i)   The case conference brings together the family and professionals concerned with child protection.
(ii) It provides a forum for sharing relevant information and analysing risk.
(iii) Its members make a decision about the need for registration.
(iv) It provides an opportunity to identify and record a child protection plan and a core group of professionals to carry it out.
(v)   It provides an opportunity to identify a key worker who can co-ordinate the multi-agency assessment, planning and review of the case. (*Working Together Under the Children Act*, 1989)

The child protection case conference is central to the child protection process and education staff should not make unilateral decisions concerning the level of risk to a child. The responsibilities of school staff are clear:

(i)   To recognize and refer any outward signs of abuse, changes in a child's behaviour and signs of a failure to develop.

(ii) To monitor and record the attendance and development of children for whom child protection procedures have been followed.

(iii) To help children acquire knowledge and develop skills through the personal and social curriculum to help them maintain personal safety. (*ibid.*)

Finally it is important to remember that schools and the staff in them can and do make a difference to whether or not a child is significantly harmed by the abuses they suffer at the hands of their parents or carers or whether they survive those abuses.

Acknowledgments

I am indebted to Jane Oulton, Team Manager (Family Support Team), Manchester Social Services Department and Sue Edmundson, Educational Psychologist, Stockport for all the work we did together at the start of this project on emotional abuse.

References

ADCOCK, M., WHITE, R. and HOLLOWS, A. (1991) *Significant Harm*, Significant Publications.

BRASSARD, M.R., GERMAIN, R. and HART, S.N. (1987) *The Psychological Maltreatment of children and Youth*, Oxford, Pergamon Press.

BUTLER SLOSS, L.J. (1988) *Report of the Inquiry into Child Abuse in Cleveland 1987*, London, HMSO.

CHILDREN'S LEGAL CENTRE (1988) *Child Abuse Procedures: The Child's Viewpoint*, Children's Legal Centre.

COVITZ, J. (1986) *Emotional Child Abuse: The Family Curse*, Sigo Press.

CREIGHTON, S.J. (1992) *Child Abuse Trends in England and Wales 1988–1990*, NSPCC, Policy, Practice, Research Series.

DES (1988) *Circular 4/88: Child Protection, Guidance for LEAs*, London, HMSO.

DHSS (1974) *The Maria Colwell Report*, London, HMSO.

DHSS (1980) *Child Abuse: Central Register Systems*, London, HMSO.

DOH (1991) *The Children Act 1989*, London, HMSO.

EDMUNDSON, S. and COLLIER, P. (1993) 'Child protection and emotional abuse: Definition, identification and usefulness within an education setting', *Educational Psychology in Practice*, **8**, 4, pp. 224–30.

EEKELAAR, J. and DINGWALL, R. (1990) *The Reform of Child Care Law. A Practical Guide to the Children Act 1989*, London, Routledge.

GARBARINO, J., GUTTMAN, E. and SEELEY, J.W. (1989) *The Psychologically Battered Child*, San Francisco, CA, Jossey-Bass.

Home Office, DOH, DES and Welsh Office (1991) *Working Together Under the Children Act 1989: A Guide to the Arrangements for Inter-Agency Cooperation for the Protection of Children from Abuse*, London, HMSO.

JONES, C. and NOVAK, T. (1991) 'Soapbox', *Social Work Today*, **12**, pp. 22–3.

LAUER, J.W., LOURIE, I.S., SALUS, M.K. and BROADHURST, D.D. (1979) *The Role of the Mental Health Professional in the Prevention and Treatment of Child Abuse and Neglect.* Washington, DC, US Department of Health, Education and Welfare.

O'HAGAN, K. (1993) *Emotional and Psychological Abuse of Children*, Milton Keynes, Open University Press.

OPEN UNIVERSITY (1989) *P554 Child Abuse and Neglect: An Introduction*, Milton Keynes, Open University Press.

ROYAL COLLEGE OF PSYCHIATRISTS, (1982) 'Definitions of emotional abuse', *Bulletin of the Royal College of Psychiatrists*, May, pp. 85–7.

RUTTER, M. (1979) 'Protective factors in children's responses to stress and disadvantage', in KENT, M.W. and ROLF, J.E. (Eds) *Primary Prevention of Psychopathology, Vol. 3: Social Competence in Children*, Hanover, NH, University Press of New England.

Chapter 5

Integrating Children with Emotional and Behavioural Difficulties: The Effect on Self-esteem

John Banks

Integration, 'Labels' and Statements in a Changing Context

In 1994 schools find themselves in a social and economic context which radically challenges previously held concepts regarding their very function as educational and pastoral organizations. At the centre of the debate is the politically derived pressure on headteachers and school governors to be subject to 'market forces' and to be economically independent of local government, hence the impetus for some to seek 'grant maintained status' (GMS). To date the 'take up' rate for GMS has been slow but under the arrangements for 'Local Management of Schools' (LMS) even those schools remaining within local authority control are now to be viewed as medium-sized businesses with substantial income, capital, assets and liabilities. Headteachers are constrained to maximize their existing resources supplementing them wherever possible by any means available. This regularly has the effect of forcing schools to make unpalatable choices between what they *can* and what they would *like* to offer pupils, not on educational grounds but according to financial considerations. If we are to be influenced by government rhetoric, the 'success' of schools as educational establishments is to be judged publicly according to politically expedient measures such as spurious 'league tables', truancy figures and exclusion rates. Within such a context the special educational needs (SEN) sector is the most susceptible to controversial change, since it potentially involves the greatest liability to examination results and the greatest pressure on school finances.

Government response to *Getting in on the Act*, the 1992 Audit commission/HMI report on the working of the 1981 Education Act (DES, 1992), has been to propose substantial amendments designed to make access to SEN provision less problematic while theoretically keeping within the spirit of the act. Section III of the 1993 Education Act, which came into effect on September 1 1994, will replace the 1981 Act, extending parent's rights and placing clearly defined duties on LEAs, schools and other professionals. These duties are outlined in the Code of Practice (DFE, 1994) and are designed to improve service delivery to children who experience special educational needs. However, it remains to be seen whether this improved service delivery will benefit *all* children who experience special educational needs.

The emotive power of making provision in mainstream for pupils with physical difficulties is readily observable and the effect of pressure groups, such as those that exist for children with Down's syndrome etc, is likewise hard for schools to resist. However, for those children who are perceived as presenting problems to the maintenance of order and discipline in schools, the picture is somewhat different. Such children are all too often simply labelled as 'disruptive', 'disturbed' or 'disordered' without adequate consideration for their emotional and behavioural difficulties (EBD) and there are legitimate concerns amongst professionals and parents with regard to the actual intentions and motives of some schools. It has been argued that some have a perception that referral for formal assessment should ideally lead to 'statements' confirming their own predetermined judgment that the child is 'ineducable' in the mainstream context. The referral therefore constitutes an important step in affording the child 'education elsewhere'. 'Market forces' compel schools to prioritize, to target resources to those pupils judged to have greatest need and very rarely do EBD pupils benefit as they should. 'Why should we spend money on pupils whose behaviour is unacceptable?' has been a query often heard by this author! When schools, who subscribe to the view implicit in such questions, are asked to make assessments in accord with the Warnock stages, problems are often defined in terms of a child's inability to cope with the curriculum offered even though no attempt has been made to modify or differentiate it. By labelling the child 'EBD' there is a hidden agenda with an inference that he needs to go to a special school, 'for his own good', and an implication that the cause of the problem lies solely within the child rather than in an interactive process between child and environment. Such schools seek to exonerate themselves from their share of responsibility, both for the current problem and for developing resources in order to provide the curriculum necessary to avoid a repetition. As a consequence of such tactics the child is branded as a failure; it is he/she who is seen as responsible for the problem regardless of antecedents and setting conditions. The implications for the child's self-esteem are obvious! In the light of recent publicity about 'league tables' and the effect of 'disruptive pupils' on the marketability of a school's public image, and as new regulations regarding exclusions make it harder to brush difficulties 'under the carpet', attempts to remove children who experience EBD from mainstream schools appear to be on the increase. A marked rise in the number of exclusions since the implementation of the 1988 Act is already observable (West, 1991; Pyke, 1991). It is also significant that requests to Educational Psychology Services for formal assessments under the 1981 Education Act continue to increase despite considerable amounts of money being delegated from LEAs to schools as a result of arrangements for LMS.

Integration and EBD

In the 1980s, a decade ostensibly characterized by integration, children who experienced emotional and behavioural difficulties did not benefit as they might from initiatives and advances enjoyed by other pupils experiencing special educational needs. The proportion of children in segregated SEN settings has generally decreased since 1983 with the exception of those experiencing EBD where the reverse is true (Goacher *et al.*, 1988). Swann (1991) found that LEAs in England provided special school places for a total of 98,441 children over 5 years old in January 1990, 1.59 per cent of the school population, compared with 1.72 per cent in 1982. However the number of children experiencing EBD who were placed in special schools and 'units' over a similar period *rose* substantially (HMI, 1989).

Labelling children as 'disruptive' and placing them in units without formal assessment or statements has continued to be an expedient way for schools to minimize expenditure on children who experience EBD, disguising the real needs and disregarding inadequacies in their own school systems. Although 'on-site' units can be an effective and positive resource, all too often they function as 'sin bins' within which access to the curriculum is restricted. It is possible that, since every child now has a right to the National Curriculum under the 1988 Act, inappropriate use of units will decrease. However, since one suggested criterion under Section 19 of the Act allows for 'disapplication' in cases where a child's conduct prevents other children from benefiting from the National Curriculum (cf DES, 1989) some schools may continue as before, by taking advantage of this 'loophole'. (Further discussion regarding the use and misuse of Section 19 may be found in Randall, 1991; and Hayes, 1991.)

Children who experience EBD have special educational needs as real as any other group but currently these are being largely overlooked. Their difficulties involve not only curriculum and resource issues but more fundamentally, the policies, approach and ethos of LEAs and schools. Some observers suggest that schools need to be more introspective:

> Children with complex social and emotional difficulties need schools which will understand and make allowances for idiosyncratic, apparently anti-social and sometimes eccentric forms of self expression; schools which understand that the origins of disaffection and low motivation can lie as much within the school as within the child or the family; schools which aim to raise low morale and damaged self esteem as much as academic attainment. (Mittler, 1990)

In looking for guidance from the DFE, schools and LEAs have found that emphasis is not on the wider needs of children who experience EBD but on 'discipline in schools', as in the Elton Report (Elton, 1989). This is perhaps characteristic of a philosophy which often views children who experience emotional and behavioural difficulties as 'naughty' and requiring 'management' rather than as people with complex needs. One positive short term consequence of the Elton Report, however, is that Education Support Grants (ESGs) were made available to LEAs for use in initiatives regarding 'discipline in schools'. Some forward looking authorities have allocated this money to multidisciplinary teams who work with schools to maximize their provision for EBD pupils in mainstream and to help make pastoral and SEN systems more effective (see Samson and Hart's chapter in this volume for for a desciption of such an initiative in action). The ESGs represent a useful, if temporary, supplement to the rapidly diminishing centrally controlled LEA monies (Banks, 1991). Such constructive use of extra financial resources is congruent with an ideology present among some educationalists which suggests that schools should ideally offer all children unlimited resources in order for their special educational needs to be met. The new duties on schools in the 1993 Education Act to make effective use of their own and the LEA's SEN resources may serve as a first step toward this goal. If resources were freely available and effectively used it could be argued that no child would have needs; we only need something if it is absent and hence the concept of special educational *needs* is based on a deficit model. It can be implied, therefore, that *need* only arises when there is a mismatch between the curriculum and resources on offer and the stimulus required to help a child develop his or her full potential.

Mainstream Support for Pupils Experiencing EBD

Encouragingly, there are still many schools who strive valiantly to meet the needs of all their children by making effective use of their own existing resources. Despite the financial and political pressures, accompanied by the plethora of current and proposed changes in legislation, they are trying to meet their responsibility to children who experience EBD by utilizing centrally funded support services and by using outreach workers from special schools to both maintain and even reintegrate children. Government preference for support team projects as cost effective provision was communicated in DES Circular 7/91 paragraphs 108 and 109 where LEAs are urged to continue such provision under LMS arrangements. The Elton Report (Elton, 1989) highlights the need for effective classroom management at the top of a list of recommendations for dealing with problem behaviour, with the INSET for teachers provided by such support teams. The failure to discuss how the advocated expansion in support services could be achieved under the LMS budget constraints is perhaps due to the Elton Committee's political sensitivities rather than oversight. The continued delegation of resources directly to schools could threaten the very existence of centrally funded support services who help schools deal with behaviour problems. Since LEAs are currently reviewing provision in terms of what they have and what they can keep under LMS (Banks, 1991), they should seize the opportunity to reorganize, rationalize and make support services more effective. But when the ultimate determinant of change is 'hard cash', what price innovation and development?

Self-esteem and EBD

Bandura (1977) argues that how an individual feels about him/herself is a powerful influence upon his/her behaviour; in other words self-esteem effects behaviour. He believes that the development of self and the behaviour exhibited, are both heavily influenced by the 'models' children observe and the reinforcement they encounter in their relationships with adults. He summarizes:

> In the social learning view . . . psychological function is explained in terms of a continuous reciprocal interaction of personal and environmental determinants. (Bandura, 1977, p. 11)

It follows that a child's perception of an adult's behaviour, together with the significance of that person to the child, is likely to determine the probability of that behaviour being copied. This may be regardless of its social desirability and positive or negative consequences. With all children, the concept of 'modelling' is a key element in the relationship between self-esteem and behaviour but with children who experience EBD, many of whom have been denied consistent appropriate models in their family environment, the provision of such models by teachers and other adults significant to the child assumes added importance, especially when trying to effect behavioural change. Often the major educational problems experienced by such children are family based (Lennox, 1991), with the ramifications of negative, inappropriate or absent models figuring prominently, together with inconsistency in parental expectations. Coopersmith (1967) argues that parents should place 'reasonable' demands on behaviour, giving the child obvious boundaries and guidelines and thus making him more likely to develop feelings of self worth. In the present author's experience, children who feel both valued and valuable tend to have parents with definite beliefs and expectations which are communicated consistently but are not enforced punitively. When sanctions are needed the behaviour is punished and not the person; the inappropriate action is seen as 'naughty', not the child and thus self-esteem is not adversely affected. Such an approach should also be at the heart of an effective teacher's interaction with all children but especially with those experiencing EBD. Coopersmith (1967) asserts that as long as the limits placed on behaviour are understood and are appropriate to the child's developmental level, then enforcing them provides the child with:

> a sense that norms are real and significant . . . (and) . . . contributes to self-definition and increases the likelihood that the child will believe that a sense of reality is attainable.

There is an implication that a child in such a situation will be less likely to have his self-esteem unduly affected by subsequent adversity and will be less likely to adopt defence mechanisms when coping with set-backs when they arise.

Similar basic principles for teachers working with children who experience EBD are described by Dolce (1984). Fairness, honesty, clarity, and patience are identified as key teacher attributes in efforts to enhance self-esteem. Teachers are also advised to have clear and definite goals utilizing a workable and suitable reward system, liaising closely with parents. Such principles are well known and are reinforced by Witter (1988) who asked 119 children and twenty teachers from EBD residential schools to evaluate teacher strategies that might be helpful in enhancing self-esteem. The teachers' and pupils' evaluations were compared. Strategies associated with a structured, well-controlled environment, with emphasis on encouraging academic attainment recognized by significant adults, were viewed as constructive by all the subjects but particularly by pupils with low self-esteem. Significantly, in accord with Coopersmith's observations above, strategies associated with lack of structure and control, with permissiveness, and instant material rewards, were perceived by all the subjects as being least likely to improve self-esteem.

While it is recognized that a child's behavioural difficulties may be a symptom of existing self-esteem problems which could be helped within an appropriate special school setting, any feelings of 'blame' resulting from the way in which problems are identified and described, may reduce self-esteem still further unless handled with sensitivity. The child may see the school's treatment of him/her as a rejection from 'normal' society which threatens to separate him/her from friends and the opportunities enjoyed by peers. In addition, the criteria for placement in special educational needs facilities are unclear to the extent that children with very similar needs receive widely varying provision. The basic unfairness of this is acutely sensed by children and their families and may lead to a negative effect on self esteem. It is has been suggested by some educationalists that the degree of rejection experienced or perceived may be related to the nature of the special educational provision made, contending that the further from the mainstream situation the child is placed, the greater may be the initial feelings of rejection. A corollary of this is a view which holds that the closer to mainstream education a child is, the higher will be his/her self-esteem. This may in effect be minimising the contribution that 'special schools', and other forms of special needs support, can make to the psychological well being of individuals in their care. A child's self-esteem may in fact be boosted as a result of appropriate placement in a segregated setting, in a caring environment among others experiencing similar difficulties, with suitable curricula and social opportunities and where he is not highlighted as being 'a problem'. However, in the present political and financial climate, there is always the worry that some schools' insistence that a child needs 'education elsewhere' may be indicative of an educational apartheid philosophy which sees SEN pupils, especially those experiencing EBD, as second class citizens who are not economically attractive in a school with control of its own finances.

Research into the interrelationship between integration and self-esteem in children who experience emotional and behavioural difficulties is notable by its sparseness. In a review of research findings related generally to self-esteem enhancement and behaviour in children Gurney (1987) notes that high levels of self esteem are:

> positively associated with better adjustment (Williams and Cole, 1969) more independent and less defensive behaviour (Rosenberg, 1965), less deviant behaviour (Fitts, 1972), greater social effectiveness (Shrauger and Rosenberg, 1970) and greater acceptance of other people (Suinn and Geiger, 1965). Moreover, in the context of the school, self-esteem has also been positively associated with school achievement (Purkey, 1970; Brookover, 1964; Simon, 1975). (p. 130)

In one of the few UK studies available, Lund (1987) found that the self-esteem of children in EBD day schools was significantly lower than that of children in mainstream implying that placement in a special school environment did not appear to enhance self-esteem. Other findings in Lund's research support the need to tailor therapeutic approaches in EBD day schools for eventual integration into the mainstream and to explore ways in which curriculum content can improve self-esteem. However, where placement of a child in segregated provision is felt to be appropriate to the child's needs, the importance of early transfer is emphasized to improve the future chances of reintegration. Where early reintegration is not possible Lund (1989) found in a separate study that children who attended EBD day schools increased their self-esteem to a non — significant degree over a two-year period, as measured by the Lawrence self-esteem questionnaire ('Lawseq', Lawrence, 1982) but the data does suggest that the schools may help increase pupil self esteem in the long term.

A small scale study by the present author (Banks, 1992) investigated the hypothesis that the self-esteem of children with the same special educational needs label, (EBD), for whom different provision is made, may be associated with their relative degree of segregation. Pupils in the following three types of provision were studied.

(i) MAINSTREAM — children identified as experiencing emotional and behaivioural difficulties but whose needs were being met from within the mainstream school's own resources without 'statements'.
(ii) SEGREGATED — pupils attending an EBD day special school.
(iii) OUTREACH — children who have been in segregated provision but who are in the process of reintegration, supported by a specialist teacher from an EBD day school.

Using a battery of self-esteem and social skills tests, interviews and case study information, evidence was collated suggesting an association between the type of provision a child receives and self-esteem. However, self-esteem did not follow a continuum based on distance from mainstream, as might have been expected, but was generally lowest in those children in the process of reintegration. Detailed scrutiny of the results revealed that children in the OUTREACH group had the lowest mean self-esteem scores on the inventories used and were also most at risk of adjustment difficulties according to the Rogers Personal Adjustment Inventory (Jeffrey, 1984). The latter finding is confirmed by the children's responses to the 'Social Situations Problem Checklist' (Spence, 1982) where they indicated twice as many problems as the MAINSTREAM group and a third more than the SEGREGATED. There is insufficient evidence to say conclusively whether the relationship is 'causative' but analysis of individual cases strongly suggests that it may be.

Implications for Practice

Available research tends to indicate that where possible children who experience EBD should be educated in mainstream contexts if their self-esteem is not to be negatively effected. The results of the Banks (1992) study give cause for concern since the outreach pupils were, until quite recently, in segregated provision where careful consideration was given to the 'within child' criteria for selection for reintegration. Teachers in the special school stated that in order to be considered for reintegration, not only do a child's emotional and behavioural difficulties have to be ameliorated to the extent where they are manageable in a mainstream situation, but the levels of social competence and self-esteem also have to be judged high enough for the reintegration to have 'a good chance of success'. Put simply, the children who are placed 'on outreach' are those who are most successful in the special school. This begs a question as to what causes these children to go from being in such a position of prominence in terms of self-esteem and social skills in one situation to a position where they have difficulties in those same personal areas in another.

On the Outside Looking In?

It is common practice for the point of reintegration to be timed for the end of year 6 so that the child can get the 'feel' of mainstream education and renew or establish friendships before transition to secondary school in year 7. Attendance is often initially part time, which would appear at first to be logical, but parents and children frequently report this to be an extremely stressful experience. The natural curiosity of the other pupils and some teachers to know the outreach pupils' background often forces them into awkward situations causing them to feel even more of an outsider than they were already. Parents interviewed by various authors report that in retrospect they would have been happier if reintegration had taken place on a full-time basis at the beginning of year 7, although at the time they were glad to see any time their child spent in a mainstream school as progress. Samson and Reason (1988) wonder if the purpose of part-time reintegration is perhaps really to reassure mainstream teachers that they can cope with the reintegrating pupil's presence! Teachers receiving a child into mainstream usually liaise with the EBD school but in many cases have not had the opportunity to work with him/her in the special school either to get to know him/her or see him/her in an environment where he/she is successful. The mechanics of the reintegration are often left to the outreach worker whose extensive brief includes responsibility for matching curricula, 'building the bridges', liaising with home and supporting the child within a very limited time allocation. In a 'perfect' situation the more experienced and effective outreach workers use the available time to support and 'skill up' the teacher, acting in a consultation model, having relatively little direct contact with the child but being on hand to help with problems if they arise. Sadly such ideal scenarios occur infrequently due to competing demands and lack of resources which inevitably endangers the success of the reintegration.

'Goods on Approval?'

In the Banks (1992) study parents reported that their children appeared happier in themselves before being reintegrated and there was a feeling expressed separately both by parents and teachers alike, that while being reintegrated children are effectively 'on parole', a situation which causes them to feel they belong neither to the mainstream or EBD school. Some teachers clearly have negative expectations of the reintegrating pupil, labelling him/her and communicating unconstructive attitudes based on limited understanding of a child's history and needs. This undoubtedly contributes to the levels of stress experienced and lowering of self-esteem. Outreach support for reintegration is usually scheduled to last for at least one full term and usually two. Parents and teachers in EBD schools generally see this in a positive light as a precaution in case the child can not settle at the new school but many mainstream teachers and the children themselves may perceive themselves as being 'on approval', to be returned if they were 'not satisfactory'. Samson and Reason (1988) observe:

> Needless to say, 'on trial' arrangements added to the stresses of transfer if the pupils perceived them as equivalent to being on parole. The practice seemed to be based on a misunderstanding of the safeguards provided by statements of special educational needs which, reviewed regularly, should have ensured additional mainstream support when necessary. (p. 21)

Children who experience EBD in mainstream and those being reintegrated from EBD schools should be supported within whole school policies which are in turn supported by either EBD outreach workers or independent peripatetic support teams. However, differences in practice may arise since the former tend to have relatively limited recent mainstream experience and the latter little involvement in special schools. In view of the continuum of emotional and behavioural difficulties LEAs with such parallel resources should be encouraged to merge them as one autonomous team serving children in both special and mainstream schools. Such an independent support team may advise the school; work with whole classes or groups; support individual pupils and teachers, provide relevant INSET; assist in selecting the most appropriate mainstream setting for a reintegrating child and fulfil an important role in designing and supporting reintegration programmes. If centrally funded they could be seen as part of the normal provision which all secondary schools could offer and thus react rapidly to referrals, hopefully meeting needs at an early stage. The 'on approval' situation mentioned above could be avoided if such a team existed. The team would already have been involved in the reintegration, as indicated above, and would be on hand to help with setbacks should they occur. The reintegrating pupil would be on a similar footing to his peers with the move from EBD school perceived as a definite, positive decision rather than 'testing the water'. LEA policy with regard to segregation would be effected since the existence of such a team could obviate the need for some pupils to leave mainstream schools in the first place. The independent status of the team could also help to prevent schools from 'off-loading' commercially unattractive pupils, especially if LEA guidelines insisted that schools refer such pupils for an 'evaluative' intervention which, if necessary, could contribute to a statement of special educational needs.

A high priority in designing support and reintegration programmes would be to ensure that self-esteem enhancement was facilitated. 'Positive monitoring systems' have a role to play in communicating a child's success not only to parents and teachers but also to himself and are in accord with Coopersmith's (1967) assertions on the benefit to self-esteem of limits placed on behaviour mentioned earlier. Further benefits could be achieved by avoiding the unnecessary highlighting of 'reintegrating' pupils and encouraging feelings of belonging within a whole school approach which prizes the value of individuals, regardless of their special needs and differences. This has implications for the way in which pastoral care, special educational needs provision and the curriculum in general, interrelate and ideally are combined into one cohesive whole. Marland (1989) stresses the need for schools to implement what he calls the 'pastoral curriculum' describing its content as:

> the task of enabling young people to understand themselves and their relationships, and to take as much as possible of their own life into their own hands. Thus knowledge, skills, sensitivity and decision making are inextricably linked and the four bound together by a growth in self esteem.

He feels that the guidance role, particularly important to the 'reintegrating' child, can not be separated from the teaching of facts, attitudes and skills. Thus subject lessons would have pastoral objectives with issues such as sex, health, multicultural and moral education weaving their thread throughout the whole school experience. Perhaps if more schools took this approach instead of paying lip service to the Education Reform Act's requirement to '... promote the spiritual, moral, cultural, mental and physical development of pupils ...' (DES, 1988, section 1 para. 2) by merely allocating one or two periods per week to 'PSE', the process of reintegration may be less difficult. The Elton Report (Elton 1989) also emphasized the importance of the pastoral curriculum particularly in preventing problem behaviour while, Marland (1980) in an earlier work asserts that:

> unless we have an agreed background curriculum, we are depending
> on children having crises before we can offer them help ...

Children who have experienced the rejection of being excluded from the mainstream system once already can do without further crises!

The Cauldron of Abundance — Concluding Thoughts

In a recent report from the Centre for Studies on Integration in Education based on DFE statistics Swann (1992) shows that nine years after the 1981 Education Act obliged LEAs to reduce segregation, the proportion of primary aged children in special schools in England was increasing. Between 1988 and 1991 the rise in this group was more than 2 per cent while at the same time the proportion of secondary age children in special schools fell by over 2 per cent making for an overall drop in segregation by 3 per cent. These figures, however, hide wide variations in practice amongst LEAs. For instance thirty-one authorities actually increased their proportion of 5–15-year-olds in special schools, one LEA by 19.2 per cent! One possible explanation is that primary schools are identifying children experiencing SEN at an early age as a consequence of the Standard Assessment Tests and the implementation of the National Curriculum and are therefore attempting to meet the pupils needs as soon as possible. More cynically, Swann (1992) suggests that schools may in effect be moving pupils into special schools to protect their own public image, academic record and ambitions while avoiding meeting the needs of 'expensive' or 'difficult' pupils.

It follows from arguments such as this that schools may be less likely to want to reintegrate such pupils unless they bring adequate funding and resources with them. *Getting in on the Act* (DES, 1992) recognizes the funding inadequacies that have existed since the 1981 Act was implemented; that these inadequacies were complicated further by the 1988 Act; and that there has been a failure to allocate specific resources for pupils with special educational needs. They identify in particular two financial factors which could be preventing effective reintegration of children into mainstream schools. These are: (i) that special schools usually hold on to the extra resources even when a child is reintegrated; and (ii) that staffing levels in the special schools have not dropped in line with the fall in pupil numbers over the last five years. Assuming a uniform situation across England and Wales, the report estimates that £53 million could have been released for integration programmes! In spite of these extra resources allegedly enjoyed by special schools, the report argues that the learning experience for children with special educational needs is virtually the same in mainstream and segregated settings. If this really is the case then it is easy to understand the wish of the 33 per cent of parents who want their child to be moved, most to a mainstream school, especially since the report suggests that the cost of educating a child in an integrated mainstream setting is no more than it would be in a special school. While commending the majority of schools and LEAs for their progress on integration the report calls for the 'strengthening' of mainstream schools to increase their capability to provide for pupils with special educational needs. It would appear that the government has taken heed of the Audit Commission/HMI recommendations and the statistical trends identified in the CSIE report (Swann, 1992) in constructing the 1993 Education Act. Parents should have greater rights as to the choice of school, in line with those whose children do not have special educational needs and the Act should improve mainstream schools' and LEAs ability to deliver special educational needs provision in locations most appropriate for the individual child as long as the will is there. However, as with its predecessor in 1981, the 1993 Education Act is to come into force with no extra funding to support it. Perhaps research should be undertaken to discover the whereabouts of an educational version of *The Cauldron of Abundance* which in Celtic legend never needed replenishing no matter how much was taken out!

References

BANDURA, A.(1977) *Social Learning Theory*, London, Prentice Hall.

BANKS, J.H.M. (1991) '*Peripatetic support services for pupils experiencing emotional and behavioural difficulties in mainstream schools*', unpublished MEd thesis, University of Liverpool.

BANKS, J.H.M. (1992) '*Self esteem in children experiencing emotional and behavioural difficulties in integrated and specialised settings*', unpublished MSc thesis, University of Manchester.

COOPERSMITH, S. (1967) *The Antecedents of Self Esteem*, London, W.H. Freeman.

DES (1981) *Education Act*, London, HMSO.

DES (1988) *Education Reform Act*, London, HMSO.

DES (1989) *Circular 22/89: Assessments and Statements of Special Educational Needs*, London, HMSO.

DES (1992) *Getting in on the Act — Provision for Pupils with Special Educational Needs: The National Picture*, London, HMSO.

DFE (1994) *Code of Practice on the Identification and Assessment of Special Education Needs*, London, Department for Education Publications Centre.

DOLCE, R. (1984) 'Being a teacher of the behaviour disordered', *Education*, **105**, 2, pp. 155–61.

ELTON, LORD (1989) *Discipline in Schools*, London, HMSO.

GURNEY, P.W. (1987) 'Changing children's overt behaviour related to self-esteem by the use of behaviour modification', *Educational Psychology*, **7**, 2, pp. 91–102.

GURNEY, P.W. (1988) *Self Esteem in Children with Special Needs*, London, Routledge.

GOACHER, B., EVANS, J., WELTON, J. and WEDELL, K. (1988) *Policy and Provision for Special Educational Needs*, London, Cassell.

HAYES, S. (1991) 'Too eagerly awaited assessment?', *British Journal of Special Education*, **18**, 2, pp. 48–51.

HMI (1989) *A Survey of Provision for Pupils with Emotional/Behavioural Difficulties in Maintained Special Schools and Units*, London, HMSO.

JEFFREY, P. (1984) *Rogers Personality Adjustment Inventory — Revised Edition*, Windsor NFER/Nelson.

LAWRENCE, D. (1982) 'The development of a self-esteem questionnaire', *British Journal of Educational Psychology*, **51**, pp. 245–9.

LENNOX, D. (1991) *See Me After School*, London, Fulton.

LUND, R. (1987) 'The self-esteem of children with emotional and behavioural difficulties', *Maladjustment and Therapeutic Education*, **5**, 1, pp. 26–33.

LUND, R. (1989) 'Self-esteem and long-term placement in day schools for children with emotional and behavioural difficulties', *Maladjustment and Therapeutic Education*, **7**, 1, pp. 55–7.

MARLAND, M. (1980) 'The pastoral curriculum', In BEST, R., JARVIS, C. and RIBBINS, P. (Eds) *Perspectives on Pastoral Care*, London, Heineman.

MARLAND, M. (1989) 'Shaping and delivering pastoral care the new opportunities', *Pastoral Care in Education*, **7**, 4, pp. 14–21.

MASLOW, A. (1954) *Motivation and Personality*, New York, Harper and Row.

MITTLER, P. (1990) 'Too difficult to address?', *Times Educational Supplement*, 23 February, p. 26.

PYKE, N. (1991) 'Rise in exclusions linked with ERA', *Times Educational Supplement*, 3 May, p. 3.

RANDALL, M. (1991) 'Can section 19 be used positively?', *British Journal of Special Education*, **18**, 2, pp. 44–7.

SAMSON, A. and REASON, R. (1988) 'What is successful reintegration?', *British Journal of Special Education*, **15**, 1, pp. 19–23.

SPENCE, S. (1982) *Social Skills Training with Children and Adolescents*, Windsor, NFER, Nelson.

SWANN, W. (1991) *Variations in the Levels of Segregation in Special Schools 1982–1990*, London, Centre for Studies on Integration in Education (CSIE).

SWANN, W. (1992) *Segregation Statistics: English LEAs 1988–91*, London, Centre for Studies on Integration in Education (CSIE).

WEST, D. (1991) 'Comment: New ways to manage needs', *Times Educational Supplement*, 26 April, p. 17.

WITTER, G. (1988) 'To see ourselves as others see us', *Support for Learning*, **3**, 2, pp. 93–8.

Chapter 6

Placement and Progress in Residential Special Schools for Children with Emotional and Behavioural Difficulties

Roger Grimshaw

Introduction

Residential special schools for emotional and behavioural difficulties (EBD) have become a live issue in any consideration of the future of EBD provision in general. Scandals at particular schools, such as Crookham Court and Castle Hill, where systematic abuse was discovered, have prompted a tightening of inspection but this has not halted a growing anxiety about the future (Ogden, 1992; Brannan *et al.*, personal communication). Reports of school closures especially in schools outside the local authority sector have added new uncertainties. Behind these particular concerns lie a series of unresolved questions about the appropriateness of placements, the type of provision on offer and the extent to which these schools can be regarded as effective in dealing with the difficulties associated with children. Answers to these questions have been extremely difficult to find in the period following the 1981 Education Act, yet they have become additionally important in the cost-conscious 1990s when expenditure on residential provision looms large in local authority budgets.

If anxiety about cost has sharpened the critical scrutiny given to residential schools there have been other influences at work over this period which have shifted the terms in which they are perceived. Part of this change has been to define special educational needs more specifically in terms of a 'learning difficulty'. The 1981 and 1993 Education Acts have sought to give greater focus to the concept of need. The implication is that provision too must be tailored more exactly to individual educational need. In that context the residential component of provision would appear vulnerable to critical assessment, since the placement must be justified educationally. The DFE circular on children with emotional and behavioural difficulties (DFE, 1994) emphasizes that references to family needs or other background problems would not seem to be sufficient on their own. Questions concerning the consequences of residential education for families become more salient once the focus of need is defined in this manner. The ways in which parents and children themselves contribute to the assessment of need therefore invite closer examination.

The 1980s have been widely perceived as a period in which there were opportunities for integrating provision for special educational needs. In this respect the use of residential special schools has appeared somewhat anomalous. Work in mainstream schools to deal with indiscipline and poor behaviour has assumed increasing importance. It is now officially accepted that the conduct of children is greatly influenced by the way they are taught and by the qualities of the school as a purposeful and caring organization in which the children's own contribution is fully acknowledged (Rutter *et al.*, 1979; DES, 1989). Schools faced with problems of discipline were encouraged to look within rather than to look outward for solutions.

Superficially these conditions would seem to favour the tightening up of referrals to residential provision, encouraging a trend towards rationalization in which these schools stood very far along a finely-graduated continuum of EBD provision. In fact, it can be argued that there has been no visible evidence of such changes; indeed, rather the opposite appears to be the case. A major aspect of the problem has been the sheer scarcity of information about the population of residential schools, their philosophy and practice, and the outcomes of their work. A recent research project by the National Children's Bureau, with assistance from the University of London Institute of Education, has sought to address these issues more concretely by undertaking a study of four coeducational schools, two run by local authorities, one independent and one 'non-maintained' (that is run by a charity). While these schools did not form a representative sample of residential EBD provision, they were selected because they had distinctive theoretically-based styles of work and each could be understood as part of a network of provision. The book on which this chapter is based shed light on their role and contribution in responding to emotional and behavioural difficulties (Grimshaw and Berridge, in preparation).

Although in 1978 the Warnock Committee called for improved EBD provision, paradoxically it appears that we know less, rather than more, about what has happened since. Even an official unified listing of residential EBD special schools in England and Wales has not been readily available. A recent survey of residential EBD schools, for example, referred to about 217 establishments but appears not to have covered non-maintained schools (Smith and Thomas, 1992). Figures for the population of residential EBD schools have remained elusive, since the last official count in 1983; since then, unfortunately, we must rely on estimates. By 1986–87 it was estimated that over 11,000 children were placed in such schools (Anderson and Morgan, 1987). Using these figures as a baseline the most up to date estimate would suggest a population of 8000. To put this figure in perspective it is worthwhile comparing trends in similar provision run by social services. Here a marked decrease has taken place in the number of children in children's homes to 1000 below the estimated number in residential EBD schools. Even if we take into account a further 3000 children in specialist local authority community homes (such as those with educational facilities) it is clear that the residential EBD sector is a major provider of residential care for children with difficulties at home and in school.

While the schools' population appears to have been in decline, it is not easy to see obvious signs of a major rationalization and a movement towards integrated provision for EBD. One reason for the persistence of the residential sector has been the diversity of acceptable reasons for referral. The Warnock Report argued that residential provision was appropriate in cases of special educational need where emotional or behaviour difficulties were 'severe', or where families could not cope with a 'severe disability'. 'Poor social conditions' and 'disturbed family relationships' that exerted adverse influences on a child's 'educational difficulty' represented further criteria for placement (Cole, 1986). The official standing of even these broadly drawn criteria has not been clear-cut. As a consequence, it has not been possible to identify a straightforward specification of the circumstances in which admission to a residential EBD school might be appropriate. In particular, it has not been possible to be clear about the severity of need that would call for residential provision compared with any other form of provision.

Referral and Assessment

In investigating the referral and assessment of children it is necessary to ask about a series of needs that may lie within the range of acceptable criteria. The referral documents of sixty-seven children who had been in school for at least a year were examined for this purpose. In the absence of relatively hard and fast criteria it was more important to look at the way children's needs were profiled in descriptive terms. These do not provide a definitive picture of the children. Rather we study the labels used by professionals and administrators to make a convincing case for referral. The use of labels as ways of defining problem behaviour and legitimating decisions about children has come to the fore in educational analysis (Gillham, 1981). It is this sociological framework that allows us to explore the referral process more concretely, outlining the different contributions of the key participants.

The Education Act 1981 sets out a procedure by which schools, parents and professionals take part in a multidisciplinary assessment organized by the local education authority (LEA) and designed to identify and meet a child's special educational needs. A 'statement' about these needs is required if a child is to enter a residential EBD school. This is still the case following the implementation of the 1993 Education Act.

The children's position in the four schools studied was complicated by the fact that some children had received statements for previous placements. Nonetheless, it was surprising to find that only half the sample of sixty-seven children had a statement specifically relating to the admission. Nearly a third of children had been given a 'provisional placement' without a specific state-ment. About one in six children had no statement even after at least a year in school.

Prior to the 1993 Education Act the completion of statements within six months was officially recommended although now LEAs have a statutory duty to comply with this timescale. However, out of twenty-eight statements for which the data was available, thirteen took at least ten months to complete and four required over twenty months. There are significant implications for children's position in the fact that statements were delayed, out of date, or simply not made.

It was not apparent that pupils themselves had been encouraged to play an active part in the referral process, particularly in influencing how the problem was interpreted and in choosing an appropriate remedy. There was a frequent reference to children's low self-esteem: indeed, this seemed to be a key concept for psychologists in appraising children's attitudes. It pointed to a need for achievement and approval which a future educational arrangement should provide. However, children's own views on this were not normally recorded.

It is clear that the principle of partnership with parents marks a difference between what has been normal in special education and the more restrictive arrangements (such as care orders) possible in childcare where partnership has required authoritative endorsement in the Children Act 1989. However, the contribution made by parents at referral seems not to have made much impact. There was virtually no evidence of parental involvement in formal conferences about the statementing. In a small minority of cases, however, there was evidence of parents making comments or giving formal agreement.

Some evidence about parental perspectives at this stage was gleaned from a survey to which forty-one parents responded (61 per cent of cases). Only 40 per cent found the LEA helpful. If more help had been offered at that time, 51 per cent would have been likely to have preferred a local day school. Fifty-eight per cent felt that more help from teachers would have contributed to maintaining the children in their previous schools. There were clearly mixed views about the appropriateness of a referral to residential special education.

Labels Used in Determining Children's Needs

The schools catered for a secondary age group, the most frequent age of admission being 12 years of age. Interestingly this a year after the pivotal transfer to the secondary school system, a time when significant educational issues must be faced. The ratio of forty-five boys to twenty-two girls showed the usual pattern of male predominance, only one of the schools containing a majority of girls (Cooper *et al.*, 1991). There were eight children from minority ethnic groups, the majority being African-Caribbean or of mixed parentage — groups also prominent among those looked after by the local authorities (Rowe *et al.*, 1989).

The study of referral documents made it possible to construct for each case a profile of labels or descriptive terms associated with a range of particular needs relating to family circumstances and health, emotional and behavioural difficulties, delinquency and educational difficulties.

The extent of family needs can be indicated by children's experience of substitute care. Schools differed in the proportions of children looked after by local authorities at admission. They were an overwhelming majority in one school, mostly in 'voluntary care', but elsewhere at least 70 per cent were *not* in care. In the latter schools, at least 60 per cent were living with parents or relatives. Very few children were on the child protection register at admission. Only 21 per cent had experience of being in care for more than a year. A majority of children had not, therefore, suffered the breakdown of parenting associated with local authority care and in only a third of cases was an advisory report prepared by Social Services. This was despite the fact that Social Services were in contact with almost half the cases at admission. The findings may explain why children were not referred for residential care services by Social Services. The fact that they all qualified for residential schooling according to assessments organized by local educational authorities is therefore significant, suggesting that the criteria used were less stringent in certain respects than those adopted by Social Services.

The most common recorded family problem was an experience of membership changes affecting 21 per cent, closely followed in prevalence by a history of inadequate control and by physical abuse to the child (the latter affecting 15 per cent). The average number of family problems attributed to children was two but the range was from zero to eight — a very great difference!

The most frequent health problems were enuresis (16 per cent) and other hygiene problems. Nine per cent had defective hearing, vision or speech. Epilepsy affected 6 per cent and other chronic conditions a similar proportion. Twenty-seven per cent had at least one health impairment, indicating a definite though not highly prevalent area of need.

The most common instance of disturbing or antisocial behaviour was disruptiveness affecting 49 per cent, compared with 21 per cent involved in offending. Only 7 per cent were labelled hyperactive. In a majority of cases, however, poor relationships with peers were reported. Non-compliance at home characterized no fewer than 73 per cent. Descriptions of emotional or personal problems were presented in only 46 per cent of cases — an obvious contrast suggesting that manifest problems of control were a major impetus to admission.

Data on children's educational competencies at admission were only partially available but showed that a clear majority of the children tested performed at a reading age below 10 years. (It will be recalled that average age at admission was 12 years.) By far the most common educational problem, however, was uncooperativeness (85 per cent) followed by making trouble in class (72 per cent) and poor concentration (54 per cent).

Disconcertingly, strategies in mainstream schools to deal with difficult behaviour had not been systematically applied to a large proportion of children. The most common strategy was to use a specialist teacher (16 per cent), a specialist part-time class (12 per cent) or a specialist full-time class (7 per cent). Support from an individual assistant or therapist/counsellor was minimal. Only 13 per cent had attended a day unit and only one child a day special school for EBD pupils. Thirteen per cent had been excluded from school. A gap in their schooling prior to admission affected 15 per cent, while 10 per cent had lost over six months schooling in that interval. It was difficult to identify a clear process of staged intervention through a continuum of provision. Though 46 per cent entered the residential EBD schools from other forms of special education, a substantial proportion were admitted from mainstream provision.

It was, however, common for children to have made contact with outside specialists. No fewer than 54 per cent had contact with an educational psychologist before the age of 11, while 18 per cent had similarly early contacts with speech therapists and also with Child Guidance. In all, 28 per cent had contact at some stage with Child Guidance and 27 per cent with a Child/Adolescent Psychological Service. These contacts helped confirm the perception of the children as worthy of further special assistance.

The research suggests that a child was finally labelled as 'a residential EBD' case once the psychologist was satisfied that both the school and the parents were having consistent difficulties; these difficulties were often sufficient to have prompted a clinical referral. The psychologist therefore acted as a screen for referrals which were prompted by concerns at school and at home. Admissions reflected, therefore, a social process in which some decisive action was formulated in order to address a manifest series of unresolved problems. General non-conformity of behaviour was the most common complaint. A broad conclusion is that referrals and admissions were *socially* driven rather than governed by precise considerations of clinical need and treatment (Ford *et al.*, 1982).

Variation in Residential EBD Provision

From need, we turn now to provision. Information on provision is again extremely sparse in the period following the surveys conducted at the end of the 1970s (Wilson and Evans, 1980; Dawson, 1980). The various approaches of psychotherapy and behavioural modification were documented then and are still alive now, according to the present study. Indeed, through children's needs may be diverse, it is remarkable how different the schools appeared.

- In one school, a *systems* model was adopted, emphasizing a balance of strategies, including externally certified examinations, the development of good relationships, the use of rewards, and a detailed prescription of basic care tasks. Such a systematic attempt to address

consistently a range of changing demands and expectations highlighted the managerial function rather than a definable philosophical
commitment.

- In another school, a model of *personalized group care* had been
constructed. Here the personal and individual needs of children were
emphasized. Control was considered important but applied flexibly.
The domestic units were carefully separated and differentiated to suit
children's assessed needs. The school was organized mainly through
a primary-style curriculum in which the personal relationships of children with their class teachers were a significant feature. A developmental psychology model underpinned this approach.

- In a third school, a model of *encouraged achievements* pervaded both
the care and educational dimension. Behavioural principles had influenced the development of a system of school awards for the achievement of personal targets. The prevalence of learning difficulties was
acknowledged by giving extra time and attention to basic educational
skills, and by introducing substantial resources of information technology. It was not surprising that a school manufacturing enterprise figured
as an intended focus of pride and achievement.

- In the fourth school, behavioural principles were also a powerful point
of reference but here the model was of *disciplined achievement*. A
differentiated and hierarchical house system had been devised to
change behaviour by rewarding compliance and achievement and
penalising misbehaviour. A full-scale and highly detailed 'token economy', covering both care and education, provided a basic structure
in the lower house units. Further, more refined behavioural strategies
were used in other houses. Standard criteria were applied to govern
the promotion and demotion of children from house to house, each
of which represented a clear progression in material conditions and
freedom. Organized group sessions were held daily, following, to
various degrees, the principles of 'positive peer culture', which was
the main strategy used in the highest house (Vorrath and Brendtro,
1985). Punctuality, order and supervision were important baselines for
practice. A secondary school curriculum aiming at GCSE was followed.
A behavioural philosophy was therefore central, though peer influences
were also purposefully addressed.

Accountability

'Good schools' are described as well managed (Ainscow, 1991). But what does
this mean for schools that lie in different sectors with distinctive lines of accountability? In particular, how in practical terms is the ethos of the school
defined? Asked to whom they were accountable, Heads mentioned a diverse
group — children and parents, LEAs, governors and, in the non-LEA sector,

school managers. It was explained, however, that children and parents were not significant influences on policy. Only one of the schools had an advisory council in which pupils participated. In the light of recent movements to empower 'consumers' in education, these were important findings. For local authority schools, the LEA was perceived as a source of advice rather than of policy, which one head described as 'very thin'. Governors were regarded as part of the public relations domain, though it was important to impress them, as one head explained. Management structures in the non-LEA sector created a different line of accountability. Here there seemed to be a tighter link which did not resemble the more discretionary structures in local authorities. For example, the head of the independent school had daily contact with his manager. Referring agencies were seen by one non-LEA school as making divergent demands, some with less interest than others in the progress of the child.

From this evidence it appeared that schools were able to construct what one Head called 'a total school ethos' with relative freedom. On this basis it was possible for highly distinctive regimes to appear. The organization of the school was very much a matter for autonomous professional discretion rather than being regulated by public authorities. It was especially disturbing that some LEAs placing children at a distance from their homes were reported to be taking insufficient interest in their reviews or plans.

In the light of this, it was important to discover how far the regulatory framework introduced by the Children Act 1989 had begun to exert an influence. Indeed, the new provision for surveillance of independent schools led to an inspection of one school during the research. In addition, discussions between another school and the Education and Social Services Departments of one authority were followed by the inspection of that school by Social Services. As a consequence, this particular school changed some of its procedures. It is essential to recognize that the issues of supervision and regulation apply to all such schools because they face challenges very similar to those posed by the Children Act to Social Services establishments. We have seen, for example, how the control of children has become a central feature of the new regulations and guidance following research evidence of institutional abuse. Physical restraint, for example, can only be used in situations where there is a danger to the child, other people or property (DOH, 1993). During the research, it was discovered that the schools experienced similar challenges in bringing their control practices fully in line with the spirit of the regulations and guidance. Yet it appears doubtful whether schools have had a legal responsibility in these matters equivalent to that imposed on children's homes. In view of the discretion accorded to heads in dealing with vulnerable children, a clear regulatory framework is urgently required; this must be at the forefront of attention when the consequences of recent fundamental changes in school inspection arrangements are assessed. Expert professional scrutiny is necessary not only to protect children but to establish more clearly the appropriateness of a given school ethos and to ensure that children's progress is adequately monitored, not only in individual but also in group terms. These will be areas where the new Code of Practice on special educational needs, arising from the Education Act 1993 (DFE, 1994), will be closely examined.

Progress of the Children

What special education achieves for children is a crucial question. Yet again there are very few answers to be found over recent years and we must go back nearly thirty years in some cases to find equivalent research on residential schools for difficult children (Roe, 1965; Petrie, 1962). There is however a well-established body of evidence that behaviour difficulties vary over time and that many, if not most, children considered difficult improve their behaviour (Topping, 1983; Fogelman, 1983). Questions then arise about whether residential education makes any difference, whether positive or negative, to the degree of improvement. However, the issues are wider, embracing a whole range of developmental goals for children.

In order to relate the study to a wider body of assessment research, it was decided to adapt the recent guide to assessment and action approved by the Department of Health for use with children looked after by local authorities (Parker *et al.*, 1991). The progress assessment was, therefore, concerned with medium-term outcomes — that is changes *over the past year* — that are regarded as open to practical influence. However, instead of relying on a single judgment, it was important to produce a cluster of assessments about an individual case. Care staff and classteachers, as well as each of the deputy heads responsible for care and for education, made parallel assessments, as did the children themselves.

The advantages of a multiple assessment conducted in a standardized format were that different viewpoints could be obtained and a range of specific topics could be systematically addressed. In these respects the research procedures made it possible to address the issues raised by previous labelling in more comprehensive and satisfactory ways. As in the study of initial assessment, the topics of family relationships, health, emotional and behavioural difficulties and educational progress were of special interest. By this stage the children were, on average, 15 years old.

Family Contact

Returning to the world outside school offers opportunities for children to cope without school supervision. Schools varied in offering 38-week or 52-week placements. In fact 80–85 per cent spent the three holiday periods at home over the past year. During term, however, 34 per cent visited home fortnightly or less frequently.

Maintaining contact with families has also been emphasized by the Children

Act 1989. Indeed 56 per cent of children said they missed living at home. Fifty-six per cent of children reported stable or increased contact with their mothers over the past twelve months and 40 per cent reported similarly about their fathers. Care staff reported not dissimilar proportions (64 and 40 per cent, respectively). However, they also indicated differences in these contacts among the schools; children at the school with the highest proportion in local authority care fared worst — a finding reflected, albeit less strongly, in the children's reports. Importantly, 51 per cent of parents wished to visit schools more often and 37 per cent wished school staff to make more frequent home visits.

It was disappointing to find that significantly fewer children from minority ethnic groups reported stable or improved contact with their ethnic group, thus raising questions about the location of placements.

Abuse

The general difficulties children faced during the year should not be under-estimated. Indeed, 13 per cent were reported to have suffered from suspected or confirmed physical abuse and 13 per cent similarly from sexual abuse. A total of 21 per cent were reported to have experienced suspected or confirmed abuse, whether physical or sexual. These staff reports pose unanswered questions about the perpetrators of alleged abuse and about where it took place, whether in the home or some other setting. Unfortunately this further data was not collected. However any abuse of children with special needs demands the closest attention (Kelly, 1992).

Emotional and Behavioural Difficulties

Data was also collected on children's current emotional and behavioural difficulties. According to the children themselves, their most prevalent difficulty was nailbiting (67 per cent) followed by frequent swearing (45 per cent) and making trouble in class (40 per cent). Sixteen per cent did not do what they were asked to do at home, compared with 12 per cent in school. Eighteen per cent admitted to frequently being in trouble with the law. Fifty-five per cent of children considered they were treated fairly in school; a significantly greater proportion of minority ethnic group children held this view. However, care staff reported that 4 per cent of children had definitely suffered from severe bullying, while this was suspected in 11 per cent of cases.

There was complete agreement among staff that frequent swearing was the most prevalent problem; care staff identified this in 59 per cent of cases. In the eyes of a majority of staff, the second most prevalent was disobedience at home (46 per cent of cases, according to care staff) followed by lack of concentration. According to teachers, 34 per cent of children were uncooperative in school but only 21 per cent made trouble in class. Fifteen per cent had

Table 6.1: Changes in the children's emotional and behavioural difficulties since referral

	Admission	**Follow-up**
Non-compliance at home	73 per cent	46 per cent (care staff's perception)
Non-compliance at school	85 per cent	34 per cent (teacher's perception)
Offences in previous year	6 per cent	15 per cent
Taking advantage of a boyfriend or girlfriend	6 per cent	25 per cent (deputy head, care)

committed offences in the past year and 7 per cent, according to care staff, frequently broke the law, compared with 9 per cent at admission according to the records. There were some disagreements between staffs' and children's reports about non-compliance and also, to a degree, about offending. Forty-three per cent of parents felt their children's compliance at home and general behaviour had improved over the year. Evidence about changes since referral (on average, over two years previously) is summarized in table 6.1.

When the behaviours recorded at admission were compared with those reported currently by staff, it appeared that a significant proportion of children were showing more signs of compliance at home and in school. But the rate of offending had increased, as had 'taking advantage of a boyfriend or girlfriend'. Interestingly, 10 per cent of children rated themselves as having no emotional or behavioural difficulties, compared with similar ratings of 9 per cent by care staff and 16 per cent by teachers.

Education

Data on yearly educational progress was collected but, in the case of both test results and National Curriculum attainment targets, these proved to be disparate or incomplete. Forty-six per cent of children, however, felt they were learning more in over half the National Curriculum subjects. According to teachers, 26 per cent had improved in performance to the same extent and 21 per cent in attitude. Sixty-five per cent of parents considered their children were learning more than they were a year ago.

Special Educational Needs

In order to make a general assessment, the areas of individual need identified in each child's statement were translated into specific questionnaire items. On average, regardless of the particular school, children said that 60 per cent of their areas of need had shown improvement over the year. Care staff and deputy heads of care reported a similar average improvement (69 and 68 per cent respectively), though there were significant differences among the schools' care staffs and deputy heads of care, with the 'disciplined achievement' school the most positive in its assessments. Teachers and deputy heads of teaching were only slightly less positive (55 per cent and 61 per cent, respectively). Encouragingly, 85 per cent of parents had a good opinion of the schools.

Conclusion: Assessment and Intervention to Assist Children in Need

One significant recent approach to the issue of difficult children has sought to identify the common problems of children dealt with by a variety of services such as health, education, social services and so on. It has been argued that, while services have their own definitions and procedures, the young people in forms of residential care face a range of shared difficulties (Malek, 1991).

There has, for example, been a substantial proportion of difficult children in residential care run by Social Services (DOH, 1992). One study of children's homes found the proportion to be a third, mainly adolescents presenting serious control problems in the home rather than the community (Berridge, 1985). Non-school attendance and behaviour problems in school affected significant minorities of that sample, while a small proportion had attempted suicide. Historically, a rise in the proportion of children with behavioural difficulties in 'voluntary care' arrangements has occurred — a group, incidentally, significantly represented in the present study sample (Bebbington and Miles, 1989).

There is evidence that parents' complaints about young people's difficult behaviour have been the starting point for many psychiatric admissions. Such cases have also included non-attendance at school — a significant point for the present study (Jaffa and Dezsery, 1989). Indeed, 11 per cent of psychiatric admissions in one study were referred by educational psychologists. Aggression, difficulties at school and at home, and peer group problems were frequently perceived at admission (Malek, 1991). These were precisely the most frequent characteristics identified in the formal documentation of admission to residential special provision in the present study. Though suicidal and unhappy feelings were also significantly present among the psychiatric admissions, difficult behaviour was a common finding (Beedell and Payne, 1988). These findings suggest that there should be more recognition of common areas of need which cross disciplinary boundaries. This approach is consistent with the definition of need used in the Children Act 1989 which relates to children's all-round development. Equally it is important in future that assessments contain specific information which makes possible a more coherent and precise approach to the analysis of need. A systematic approach applied in all settings would enable provision to be more carefully tailored to the identified needs.

The nature of residential EBD provision is fundamentally determined by practitioners with a variety of views about what is effective. It is important that some form of strategic oversight and regulation be introduced which can evaluate provision and assess outcomes. An interdisciplinary approach which acknowledges the common needs of children can help to bring a coordination of effort and focus on central issues such as the prevention of abuse and the promotion of good childcare practice. Hopefully the Code of Practice associated with the Education Act 1993 will mark an opportunity to consider fresh steps along this road.

If progress in various settings is assumed to occur in many, if not most, cases, the data tends to confirm this assumption for the residential schools in the study. Other studies of residential schools suggest broadly similar conclusions (Roe, 1965; Dawson, 1980; Kolvin and others, 1987). However if, as some studies argue, progress is made *irrespective* of setting, then the unique role of these schools becomes more difficult to perceive: is it really necessary to provide such a specialist resource? The answer to this question depends on a further question: how else can these children to be looked after and educated? As we saw at admission, their previous settings seemed unprepared to continue to tolerate them and alternative services were not offered in abundance. Children arrived in the schools not through rational allocation but through a process, in effect, of social exclusion. Until this issue is addressed, there can be no coherent policy for residential special education. The residential EBD schools appear to offer a setting in which some developmental tasks can be progressed when the children's families and their previous schools have reached a limit to their resources and tolerance. Policy in future needs to recognize the interdependent relationship between the residential EBD sector and the difficulties which schools and families confront. Only a systematic approach to children in need, across disciplinary boundaries, can help to clarify the future role and purpose of residential EBD schools.

References

AINSCOW, M. (1991) 'Effective schools for all: An alternative approach to special needs in education', in AINSCOW, M. (Ed) *Effective Schools for All*, London, David Fulton.

ANDERSON, E.W. and MORGAN, A.L. (1987) *Provision for Children in Need of Boarding/ Residential Education*, Boarding School Association.

BEBBINGTON, A. and MILES, J. (1989) 'The background of children who enter local authority care', *British Journal of Social Work*, **19**, pp. 349–68.

·BEEDELL, C. and PAYNE, S. (1988) '*Making the case for child psychotherapy: A survey of the membership and activity of the Association of Child Psychotherapists*', unpublished, Association of Child Psychotherapists.

BERRIDGE, D. (1985) *Children's Homes*, Oxford, Basil Blackwell.

BRANNAN, C., JONES, J.R. and MURCH, J.D. (personal communication) *Castle Hill Report: Practice Guide*, Shrewsbury, Shropshire County Council.

COLE, T. (1986) *Residential Special Education*, Milton Keynes, Open University Press.

COOPER, P., UPTON, G. and SMITH, C. (1991) 'Ethnic minority and gender distribution among staff and pupils in facilities for pupils with emotional and behavioural difficulties in England and Wales', *British Journal of Sociology of Education*, **12**, 1, pp. 77–94.

DAWSON, R.L. (1980) *Special Provision for Disturbed Pupils: A Survey*, London, Macmillan Education.

Roger Grimshaw

DES (1989) *Discipline in Schools: Report of the Committee of Enquiry* (Chairman Lord Elton) London, HMSO.

DFE (1994) *Circular on Children with Emotional and Behavioural Difficulties*, London, DFE Publications Centre.

DFE (1994) *Code of Practice on the Identification and Assessment of Special Educational Needs*, London, DFE Publications Centre.

DOH (1992) *Choosing with Care: Report of the Committee of Inquiry into the Selection, Development and Management of Staff in Children's Homes* (Chairman Norman Warner) London, HMSO.

DOH (1993) *Guidance on Permissible forms of Control in Children's Residential Care*, London, HMSO.

FOGELMAN, K. (1983) *Growing up in Great Britain*, papers from the National Child Development Study, London, National Children's Bureau/Macmillan.

FORD, J., MONGON, D. and WHELAN, D. (1982) *Special Education and Social Control: Invisible Disasters*, London, Routledge and Kegan Paul.

GILLHAM, B. (Ed) (1981) *Problem Behaviour in the Secondary School. A Systems Approach*, London, Croom Helm.

GRIMSHAW, R. and BERRIDGE, D. (in preparation) *Educating Disruptive Children: Placement and Progress in Residential Special Schools for Emotional and Behavioural Difficulties*, London, National Children's Bureau.

JAFFA, T. and DEZSERY, A.M. (1989) 'Reasons for dmission to an adolescent unit', *Journal of Adolescence*, **12**, pp. 187–95.

KELLY, L. (1992) 'The connection between disability and child abuse: A review of the research evidence', *Child Abuse Review*, **1**, pp. 157–67.

KOLVIN, I., WRATE, R.M., WOLSTENHOLME, F. and HULBERT, C.M. (1987) 'Seriously disturbed children in special settings and ordinary schools', *Maladjustment and Therapeutic Education*, **5**, pp. 65–81.

MALEK, M. (1991) *Psychiatric Admissions: A Report on Young People Entering Residential Psychiatric Care*, London, The Children's Society.

OGDEN, J. (1992) 'In the wake of terror', *Social Work Today*, **23**, 48, pp. 12–14.

PARKER, R., WARD, H., JACKSON, S., ALDGATE, J. and WEDGE, P. (1991) *Assessing Outcomes in Child Care: The Report of an Independent Working Party established by the Department of Health*, London, HMSO.

PETRIE, I. (1962) 'Residential treatment of maladjusted children', *British Journal of Educational Psychology*, **32**, pp. 27–39.

ROE, M. (1965) *Survey into Progress of Maladjusted Pupils*, London, Inner London Education Authority.

ROWE, J., HUNDLEBY, M. and GARNETT, L. (1989) *Child Care Now: A Survey of Placement Patterns: Research Series 6*, London, British Association for Adoption and Fostering.

RUTTER, M., MAUGHAN, B., MORTIMER, P., OUSTON, J. and SMITH, A. (1979) *Fifteen Thousand Hours: Secondary Schools and Their Effects on Children*, London, Open Books.

SMITH, A.S. and THOMAS, J.B. (1992) 'A survey of supportive work with the families of pupils in schools for emotionally and behaviourally disturbed children', *Therapeutic Care and Education*, **1**, 3, pp. 135–50.

TOPPING, K.J. (1983) *Educational Systems for Disruptive Adolescents*, London, Croom Helm.

VORRATH, H. and BRENDTRO, L. (1985) *Positive Peer Culture* (2nd edn), New York, Aldine Publishing.

WILSON, M. and EVANS, M. (1980). *Education of Disturbed Pupils: Schools Council Working Paper, 65*, London, Evans/Methuen Educational.

Chapter 7

Get Them Young: The Impact of Early Intervention on Social and Emotional Development

Anne Rushton

Introduction

> For under-privileged or deprived children, enriching or compensating education needs to be provided during the pre-school years. . . . Educationists are unanimous that . . . truancy . . . like teenage vandalism which leads to crime — would be reduced if children felt comfortable and confident in schools. And the way to bring that about? Break them into the system with nursery education. (Roy Hattersley, *Mail on Sunday*, November 1993)

Beneath Roy Hattersley's rhetoric and political message enshrined within it is a belief, that if children reach statutory age having the necessary academic and social skills to benefit immediately from their transition into school, they are at much less risk of failing at a later stage.

Failure within the educational system correlates highly with such negative outcomes as juvenile crime, unemployment and poverty. Along the way, failing children suffer unhappy experiences, gathering feelings of poor self-esteem and self-worth and their teachers often express their equally strong feelings of frustration and inadequacy at their inability to affect change in a positive direction.

As a practising educational psychologist, over nearly two decades, I have increasingly found teachers expressing their concerns about very young children's problem behaviour. Whilst often couched in supportive terms about the child displaying the behaviour, the not so very covert agenda is usually in relation to the impact this behaviour will have on the other children in the group. I have often sensed dislike of the children in the descriptions given by teachers and I have speculated as to what messages are conveyed unwittingly in the child-teacher transactions.

In this chapter I begin by reviewing some of the evidence on the nature and incidence of problem behaviour in young children. This is followed by a discussion on the effects of pre-school provision on children's development. I then focus on the crucial area of continuity and transition from pre-school to school and refer to the results of a small-scale study in which I have been involved. Finally I consider some promising strategies to assist this transition process and which help to prevent the development of emotional and behavioural difficulties in later childhood.

Problem Behaviour in Young Children; An Increasing Phenomenon?

The Elton Report (1989) addressed teachers' concerns that the number of children displaying verbal and physical aggression in school was increasing and that this behaviour was becoming more common amongst younger children. It suggested that some children entering nursery and reception classes 'lack the basic social skills needed to talk to and play with other children' (p. 134) and the aggressive behaviour was used 'as a substitute for other forms of communication' (*ibid.*).

Since 1989, articles in the popular press have discussed the perceived rise in difficult behaviour in school settings amongst 3–7-year-olds in terms of both frequency and severity. Young children are being described as 'hard-faced tiny terrors', 'uncontrollable' and 'abusive' and their behaviour is being blamed for teachers leaving the profession. Truancy figures tend to bear out that increasingly young children are having days and sometimes weeks out of school thus further diminishing their access to academic and social opportunities.

Children with social and behavioural difficulties, I believe, are the most discriminated against group with special needs. In a climate of change towards inclusive education, they often present the greatest challenge to the spirit of equality of access and opportunity and the eventual cost to local authorities in residential provision (the ultimate non-inclusive option) can be enormous as can the cost that being labelled 'EBD' can have on a young child's future.

In considering whether problem behaviour in young children is on the increase or changing in nature, it is important to review the range of difficult or problem behaviour that is typically observed in children at this stage in their development.

Non-compliant behaviour is relatively common among 3 and 4-year-olds (Curtis, 1986) and it is often explainable for the following reasons. The child may:

- lack understanding of the institution;
- not be sure of the behavioural boundaries;
- be accustomed to displaying emotional outbursts;
- be used to being the centre of attention;
- be overwhelmed by the hurly burly of school.

Aggressive behaviour in the form of temper tantrums, biting, hitting, fighting, shouting, swearing and threatening are also not uncommon although they may often be displayed in a specific setting (for example, temper tantrums when out shopping with a parent).

Manning and Sluckin (1984) found big differences in the amount of aggression displayed by children on entering primary school. They were able to distinguish between two types of aggression:

> Hostile aggression, where there was a definite intention to hurt and/ or to control the situation was used regularly throughout the nursery years by children who were seen as very aggressive and less able to regulate their behaviour according to the requirement of the setting. These children were usually defined as more difficult children.
>
> The second type, manipulative aggression, was seen as a strategy for attaining a specific goal (for example, getting a toy back from a child who had taken it) or for bolstering self-esteem. This was said to be displayed on occasions by less aggressive, better adapted children whose general stance was friendly, warm and positive.

Elton's estimate of one in twenty children displaying verbal aggression in school takes into consideration older children in the calculation. There is little doubt, however, that verbal aggression towards adults is more often heard in infant classes than in nursery classes.

Very young children generally show more aggression towards their peers than to adults. Language development is a limiting factor at this stage to the use of verbal aggression, but as children gain more confidence with language, it is used increasingly to self regulate and to control others. Young children may experience very strong feelings of emotional pain, anger and fear and they may 'hit out' verbally at anyone in the vicinity. A well aimed 'I wish you were dead!' for instance can be very difficult for an adult to deal with and is very attention getting for the child.

Temper tantrums, so often seen in 2 and 3-year-olds, can endure much longer in some children. This behaviour is associated with the display of other adverse behaviour traits (for example, fighting, bullying, destructive tendencies) later on. Golding and Rush (1986) who found this link, also found an incidence of 15 per cent of boys and 10 per cent of girls displaying temper tantrums in their survey of preschoolers. The incidence being higher in children living in poor inner city environments.

Richman *et al's* (1982) often cited longitudinal study of 3-year-olds highlighted that whilst it is not possible to predict with any certainty which of those who displayed problem behaviour at 3 will go on to display this at 4 and 8, certain factors were relatively more predictive. Very restless children for instance often went on to have behaviour problems and almost twice as many boys as girls continued to display problems at 8 years. Some 75 per cent of children considered to be displaying moderate to severe behaviour problems at 3 went on to show these at 8. The reasons for this continuity were not isolated however.

The literature on child development shows that some aggression in young children is to be expected as a function of their development and that it may, in certain situations, be useful to a child. As new, more effective socially acceptable strategies are mastered, assertiveness can take the place of aggression. However, during periods of uncertainty and stress in a young child's life, old familiar patterns of behaviour may reappear as regression to an earlier stage of development. For some children, transition to school is one such period of anxiety and stress.

Research Evidence on the Effects of Early Intervention

Currently much quoted in the media and in political debate, are the early intervention studies carried out largely in the United States over the last thirty years. These studies initially looked at the impact of the nursery curriculum on academic outcomes and later, other outcomes such as social behaviour were explored.

Early intervention educational programmes such as those embodied in Head Start and Follow Through showed that the nursery children that went through such programmes made initial intellectual gains in comparison to matched children who did not. However, these gains tended to 'wash out' over time and by the time children reached high school, the initial advantage they had gained had disappeared even in the most effective intervention programmes.

Some additional important findings from these studies for our consideration of children going through transition are summarized below.

1   Commitment
    Many programmes offering a change in philosophy to the norm initially give positive results but they often suffer from the 'generation effect'. In other words, they are carried by the enthusiasm of their devotees regardless of content. The enthusiasm tends to get watered down over time.

2   Continuity
    The wash out effect is stronger and happens more quickly to pre-five programmes that are not carried through into school (Farran, 1990).

3   Parental Involvement
    Programmes which involve parents from the outset tend to endure over time (Halpern, 1990).

4   Intellectual v. Social Benefits
    Although the intellectual advantage gained by children undergoing

early intervention programmes was not sustained, real *social* benefits seem to be derived which are more persistent over time.

Schweinhart *et al.* (1985) describe a follow-up study of 19-year-olds who had participated in the Perry Pre-school Study some fifteen years earlier. Of the sample of young people found who had undergone the Perry Pre-school programme, outcomes in terms of type of education, anti-social behaviour and employment were considerably more positive in this group than in a matched group who had not.

Schweinhart (op cit.) has argued that pre-school education is effective because it raises intellectual competence from the outset thus ensuring that children's early interactions with their teacher are positive leading to sustained or increased self-esteem and greater school commitment and higher academic attainment.

Schweinhart *et al.* (1986a and 1986b), along with several other studies, compared the outcomes of three different pre-school experiences on a group of 15-year-olds from low income disadvantaged families. The two experimental experiences were:

(i)   Direct Instruction — scripted, finely sequenced instructional programmes involving highly adult controlled, intensive learning experiences;

(ii) High Scope — a child initiated but adult structured learning environment involving active choice for the child, developed out of the earlier Perry Programme.

The third control group of 19-year-olds had experienced conventional nursery education.

The researchers found that the young adults who had experienced High Scope or Direct Instruction as pre-schoolers had had higher IQs at school entry than the controls. But by the time those who had experienced Direct Instruction had reached 15 they had engaged in more anti-social behaviour than those who had experienced High Scope and they had had a lower commitment to school.

Although the results are controversial, the conclusion that pre-school programmes raise initial intellectual competence within an environment of active learning rather than in a rigid adult dominated one has much support in Britain as it is in line with current philosophy much promoted within British nursery and infant classrooms. However the important point is that it appears *not* to be pre-school education per se that makes the difference, but the participation in good programmes which emphasize language and social development as well as basic skill acquisition within a context which is meaningful to the child. It is the effect of these programmes which endure over time.

In the United States, cost-benefit analyses have been carried out on many of the early intervention programmes. The evidence that early intervention with disadvantaged children increases school success (and thereby reduces the overall costs of schooling) is quite strong (Barnett and Escobar, 1990).

Although this is a complex issue, in broad terms, early programmes such as High Scope appear to have benefited the American tax payer in reduced policing, courts and prison costs and welfare payments.

American research is often quoted by the pro nursery education lobby in Britain and should appeal to any government concerned with the promotion of a nation's emotional well being. The appeal of the 'get them young' lobby is that if it is possible to 'vaccinate' a child against negative experiences by giving him/her access to nursery education, then in the long term, this would be effective in reducing the costs to society in the same way that it has in the United States.

Indeed the Elton report (1989) also summarized the USA research findings.

Large scale evaluation of pre-school education programmes for children from severely disadvantaged backgrounds indicate that such children are more likely to develop a positive self-image and to succeed at school if they have pre-school education than if they do not. Local authorities should therefore ensure that enough provision is available to meet the needs of such children. (p. 148)

This view has been strongly endorsed by the recently published report of the National Commission on Education's upon which Roy Hattersley's article was based. This called for smaller classes, better teacher training and nursery schools for *all* children.

Continuity and Progression at Transition

One important aspect of the research on early intervention has focused on the importance of maximizing the potential benefits by ensuring that the process of transition is carefully managed. Much of this work has been summarized by Tizard (1975) and Clark (1988). Continuity of curriculum and the transition process from home to pre-school provision, from home into school and from pre-school into school are highlighted as key areas of concern for all children, but more particularly for emotionally vulnerable children. For example Brown and Cleave (1991) state that:

Starting school for children is not just about having a new school bag and arriving at the beginning of the new term. The process, which should start long before the term of entry, should be given a considerably amount of thought by school staff and plans should be made which accommodate the individual needs of the children being admitted to school. Starting school is an important time for children and their parents and teachers, and an appropriate induction programme is essential. (p. 3)

The Rumbold Report (1990) was concerned with the quality of educational experience offered to 3 and 4-year-olds and reinforced many of the recommendations made by Clark's team, it underlined the need to maintain effective assessment and record keeping systems in order to ensure that continuity was achieved.

> Continuity occurs when there is an acceptable match of curriculum and approach allowing appropriate progression in children's learning. (Rumbold, 1990, p. 13)

In practice this may be difficult to achieve due to the many impinging factors influencing a child's early experiences. The range of different pre-school experiences a child may have had before 5 years of age are listed by Rumbold:

- very different settings;
- embodying different persons;
- providing different opportunities;
- presented by people with very different training.

Curtis (1986), cited by Rumbold, outlined areas of potentially disturbing discontinuity at transition into statutory education:

- changes in the physical environment and the way in which children are able to interact with it;
- differences in classroom organization, routines and expectations;
- changes in curriculum content;
- different ideologies of education in pre-statutory and statutory provision.

Barrett and Trevitt (1991), in their book on the impact of attachment on the behaviour of children in school, emphasize the need for supporting vulnerable children through changes by providing structure, predictability and sensitivity in the classroom.

> Those (children) who feel secure can negotiate transitions and tolerate stressful experiences without long-term disruption to their general development and scholastic progress. Children who are emotionally insecure and anxious are less able to overcome these difficulties and, in the extreme, become overwhelmed and lose their capacity for play and learning. (p. 25)

Douglas (1989) points out that behaviour problems in young children do not have their origins in one cause or group of causes. There are significant numbers of children who seem to be able to make progress and conform inspite of the presence of considerable stress inducing factors. These children appear to develop effective coping strategies inspite of adverse circumstances.

Rutter (1985) highlighted three key requirements for an individual in order to withstand adverse circumstances:

   (i)   a sense of self esteem and self confidence;
  (ii)   a belief in one's own self-efficacy and ability to deal with change and adaptation;
 (iii)   a repertoire of social problem solving approaches.

The role of a school in promoting and supporting the development of the above cannot be underestimated. For some children it can be arguably the counterbalance to disturbing life experiences by providing the opportunities to develop a positive perception of self and to acquire adaptive social skills. Further evidence comes from Werner (1990). He summarized findings from diverse and extensive studies across differing socioeconomic levels and in different cultural contexts. Three types of protective factors emerged consistently:

   (i)   the dispositional attributes of the child;
  (ii)   the affectional ties and socialization practices within the family;
 (iii)   the external support systems that reinforce competence and provide children with a positive set of values.

The role of the school is clearly significant:

> Research has shown in that the promotion of resilience in young children by caring adults does not rely on removing stress and adversity completely. . . . but in helping them encounter graduated challenges that enhance their competence and confidence. (*ibid*, p. 112)

He goes on to say:

> Such challenges appear to be most effective for young children in the context of an organized and predictable environment that combines warmth and caring with a clearly defined structure and an established setting of explicit limits that are consistently enforced.

Clearly such factors are more likely to impact on children with less skills to cope with the changes.

All children bring a wealth of different experiences with them when they enter nursery classes and infant schools. Figure 7.1 offers a summary of the most obvious ones. The closer the match between the child's experiences and those of the setting into which the transition is being made, the less adjustments the child will have to make. Where previous experiences are very different, children may have developed in particular areas to the exclusion of others which will need to be balanced in school. For example, the children of travelling families often develop early self-sufficiency with older children taking

Figure 7.1: Early years: children's experiences to take into consideration at transition

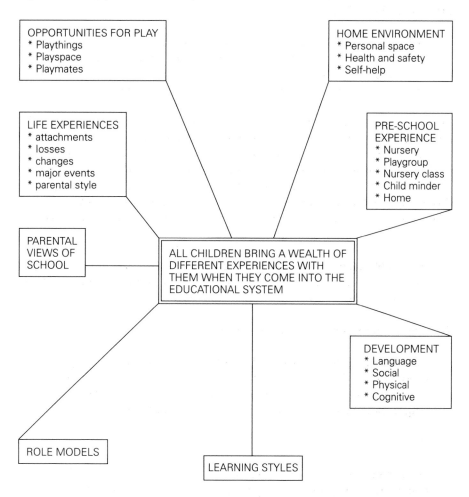

responsibility for younger children. Their play opportunities may come from improvization with naturally occurring materials, for example, bricks, sticks, puddles etc. and they may need to be guided to tune in to more academically-orientated activities, for example, listening to stories, playing concept games and following routines and time keeping. Howe (1993) points out that children unprepared for classroom learning may reach school entry:

- lacking listening skills
- lacking attending skills
- unable to make use of learning strategies (for example, rehearsal)
- lacking the various attributes that contribute to the beginnings of autonomy and self control.

I have found that such children rapidly acquire a fear of failure and often develop defensive strategies which may further exacerbate the situation for them.

Further, some children, due to local policies, enter reception class in an infant school well before their 5th birthday and are vulnerable due to the different learning needs of 4-year-olds (Brown and Cleave, 1991).

Therefore, by the time children are five years old, some may simply be non-conforming due to ignorance of the rules within the school setting. These children often come into school having already learned to behave in ways which are not acceptable in the school context. They may be disruptive, naughty, irritating to peers and adults and be overly demanding. They present problems to teachers and other children as they challenge authority with differing norms of expected behaviour from their previous experience. In familiar settings (for example, in the home), their behaviour may be quite acceptable and they would be seen as adjusted within that context.

Other children may carry emotional problems with them into all settings. They may well also display difficulties in concentrating and an inability to interact with other children but the cause of the behaviour may be rooted in traumatic or disrupted family life. Amongst this group will be children experiencing abuse or the loss by separation or death of a parent or care giver. We need to be mindful of the important emotional luggage which children bring with them into school. Careful exploration of outside school issues should help teachers to understand some of the behaviour they are dealing with and hopefully enable them to act sympathetically to the child's additional needs.

Do Different Pre-school Experiences Make a Difference?

The difference in curriculum offered in various pre-school settings has been linked to the behaviour of children at transition.

Sylva *et al.* (1980) showed significant differences between the context and nature of the input in playgroups compared to nursery classes. In her study, children in playgroup settings were typically allowed free play, punctuated by adult-led games and stories. The adults were seen to be dominating the children's activities whereas in nursery class settings, children engaged in more guided play with the adult's intervention tending to be more facilitative and extending of child initiated activities.

In a later study, Jowett and Sylva (1986) were able to show differences in the behaviour of children entering reception class from nursery and playgroup settings. The children in the study were matched for family structure, age, sex, parental occupation and were all deemed to be 'working class'. Children from nursery classes were found to be more purposeful and creative in their play than playgroup children. They showed more self initiated 'academic' type activities than their playgroup counterparts who tended to spend more time watching, looking and asking adults for help.

In addition, the children from nursery classes showed superior concentration and initially, the amount of language used was greater, although this difference disappeared after a six month period. However even after six months, the playgroup children continued to make more requests to the teacher for help and the nursery children made more contribution comments.

In a study of children in transition to reception class, Hutt *et al.* (1989) measured children's success in bidding for teacher attention. They found that children from nursery settings made more *verbal* bids for attention than did those from home. There was a large gender difference here with girls making relatively few of the bids. It was also interesting the *verbal* bids were more successful in attracting a teacher's attention than non-verbal ones.

Cleave *et al.* (1982) highlighted the gulf between pre-school and infant staff in their philosophy and purpose. She referred to pre-school staff wanting 'more contact with schools' and feeling 'their opinions are not valued' and infant staff knowing 'nothing of their new entrants pre-school experiences' and regarding 'pre-schools with suspicion', seeming 'unapproachable to parents and non-professionals' and 'unaware of the cultural customs of their pupils'.

This begs the question 'Has this gulf been bridged during the intervening decade?' More precisely 'To what extent do staff responsible for four and five year olds, share a common purpose, plan together and communicate with each other about the needs of individual children?'

Entry to reception class, therefore, is not an even race. The effectiveness of a school's social controls on individual children is going to be subtly altered by the child's previous experiences which have been determined largely by the adults he/she comes into contact with during the pre-school years.

The Management of Transition in an Inner City Area

A Small-scale Survey

A recently conducted small-scale study carried out by my colleague Irene Walker and myself looked at the policy and practice of infant schools, nursery classes and social services nurseries when planning for the transition of children from pre-school provision to school. Data was collected by questionnaire from thirty-two reception teachers, twenty-nine school nursery teachers and seven social services day nurseries in the same locality. Information was collected about current practice in relation to:

- how day nurseries, nursery schools and nursery classes prepare children for transfer to reception class;
- how the infant school plans for transition of under 5s to reception;
- how information regarding individual children's needs is communicated between concerned parties.

In this study, the vast majority of children in the area had had access to some form of pre-school experience prior to 5 and all the schools in the sample offered nursery class provision with children from day nurseries, playgroups, child minders etc. feeding into them.

Children were moved into reception classes at the beginning of the term in which they had their fifth birthday, thus some only had the experience of one full term in reception due to their birthdate being in the summer.

There is only sufficient space in this chapter to summarize the survey's main findings.

1   On the whole the transition process was viewed by staff as being a necessary hurdle to be got over as quickly as possible and then forgotten about as the 'new' process of education takes over.

2   For many children the behaviours they displayed on entry to school were indicative of emotional and behavioural disturbance. They appeared to be having problems in coming to terms with the loss of familiar settings, people and routines in the pre-school setting, particularly those children with tenuous attachments in their home environment.

3   The frequency with which children complained of physical symptoms (feeling sick) and displayed presumed attention seeking ploys increased as they moved into reception class.

4   The forging of links with parents was seldom mentioned as a priority and many staff stated that this was an area which needed to be developed.

Some Initiatives from Individual Schools at the Transition Stage

Although the findings summarized above suggest that there is a great deal that could be done to improve the transition process, the survey highlighted a range of strategies that were being adopted both in nurseries and infant schools. They deserve a mention here:

(a)   One infant school had employed a community worker to work within the nursery, running a mother and toddler group in which the focus was on promoting language development, play and independence skills prior to admission to the nursery. Staff reported an additional spin-off in the increased level of parental involvement in the children's learning and in forging good relationships between staff and parents.

(b)   One nursery school which fed into several primary schools in the area, had adopted a whole-school policy for the management of difficult behaviour using a behavioural approach with rewards for prosocial behaviour.

Children were prepared for transition, not by starting school work as such, but by developing their ability to, for instance, sit still for longer periods; get out and put away materials; answer to their names and join in and take turns in discussions. The nursery day was fairly structured with a balance struck between teacher directed and child driven tasks. Parents were encouraged to participate actively in the life of the school and in their child's learning. In addition basic education in various areas including assertiveness training was made available for them.

Since the introduction of the above in 1989, the nursery reported fewer problems with hitting, kicking, tantrums or defiance. Any new anti-social behaviours that emerge are carefully monitored and recorded and a whole school strategy for managing and reducing this is planned.

(c) The creative use of one school's delegated budget enabled extra nursery and reception staff to be deployed to ensure supported transition for the school's considerable number of children with special needs. The staff:pupil ratio was maintained at 1:15 or less, enabling weekly individual sessions to be possible with each child. Careful observations and assessments were continually made and the information was used to inform learning programmes and were passed on to parents and future teachers. A purposeful business like atmosphere was generated with on task behaviour maximized, children working independently and quietly.

The school reported significant differences in terms of use of language and cooperative learning as well as concentration in the behaviour of the children who had been part of this regime compared to those who had not. These children were perceived as noisier and less able to work independently, with less motivation.

Intervention Strategies in the Early Years

The above discussion has focused on strategies which some schools have used to facilitate the transition process. From the literature, discussions with nursery and school staff and data collected from the transition survey, I have gleaned some examples of positive practice which can be used throughout the pre-school and infant years and which are aimed helping children become adjusted to school life and less likely to display emotional and behavioural difficulties. Some of these are briefly described below.

Implementation of Early Intervention Programmes in Nurseries

High Scope nursery programmes originating from the earlier American programmes of the same name are being implemented in nursery settings across

Britain. The focus on child-directed activities within a highly structured nurs
setting has it proponents and opponents. Those involved in the initiativ
claim positive gains in children's ability to interact with their learning en'
onment in a proactive way, their actual progress in acquiring basic skills a
their developing self-esteem and cooperative behaviour.

Other projects such as the Nurture Group Initiative with its slogan 'grow
not pathology', pioneered in Inner London by Marjorie Boxall (Bennath
1993), also claim success with young vulnerable children, supported at 1
early stages of mainstream schooling.

Social Skills Training

Children entering school with underdeveloped social skills are at an obvic
disadvantage from the outset. Although friendship groups in early childho
often form and reform, it is noticeable the benefit that children with spec
educational needs in particular gain from positive relationships with their pe
and of course with the adults with whom they come into contact. By midc
childhood, a child's poor acceptance by his/her peers seems to be very stron;
linked to the likelihood of that child's involvement in juvenile delinquen
later on according to several studies.

Frederickson (1990) has suggested that social skills work involving a co:
bination of some behavioural strategies with an active problem-solving a
proach which addresses the real problems children encounter in the classroc
and playground offers the hope of reversing the above negative trends. Tl
type of work has typically been tried with junior aged children. I would arg
that an ongoing programme for all children, applied more intensively 1
children with known difficulties, should be in place during transition frc
nursery onwards.

Cooperative Learning

Reason (1991) has highlighted the importance of cooperative behaviour in
classroom setting not only for the impact that this has on the general behavio
of the class but also for the impact that these skills have on a child's academ
learning and self-esteem. She suggests strategies that can be used effective
in school settings to deal with areas of difficulty before they escalate ar
become entrenched.

There are now excellent teaching materials available to provide you
children opportunities to learn how to listen and be listened to, to take turr
to resolve conflict by negotiation and to play together without conflict. Wor
ing in cooperative classrooms can be enriching for teachers as well as childre

Assertive Discipline

Essentially a strategy employing the principles of behaviour modification, Canter and Canter's (1976 and 1984) approach to classroom discipline enabling the setting of firm, consistent limits in the context of a positive and supportive relationship between teacher and child is being used extensively in certain schools. Appropriate strategies are suggested for use with younger children and the predictability and clarity of expectations can be very helpful for children with social learning needs.

Concerns about this method, however, focus on the limitations it tends to impose on social interaction between children and the lack of opportunities children have to make choices in the learning environment.

All the above strategies are inevitably affected by human and economic resource issues and it remains to be seen whether the positive benefits reported endure over time.

The Impact of the Code of Practice

The 1993 Education Act's new Code of Practice (DFE, 1994) contains suggestions for good practice in relation to children with special educational needs undergoing transition to primary school. Figure 7.2 summarizes the broad

Figure 7.2

THE CODE OF PRACTICE

MOVING TO PRIMARY SCHOOL: CHILDREN WITH IDENTIFIED OR
POTENTIAL SPECIAL NEEDS

The headteacher, special educational needs coordinator and the child's classteacher should:

- use information arising from the child's early years experience to provide starting points for the curricular development of the pupil;
- take appropriate action, for example developing an individual education plan and monitoring and evaluation strategies to maximize development and alert any relevant support or external professionals at the earliest possible stage;
- ensure that ongoing observation and assessment provides regular feedback to teachers and parents about a child's achievements and experiences and that the outcomes of such assessment form the basis of planning the next steps of a child's learning;
- use the assessment process to allow children to show what they know, understand and can do as well as to identify any learning difficulties;
- involve parents in developing and implementing the learning programmes at home and in school.

---

recommendations. Children with social and behavioural difficulties will undoubtably benefit from the implementation of these.

The Code promotes the principle of early identification of special educational needs and early intervention, it also emphasizes the importance of close working relationships with parents and the vital role they should play. Brown and Cleave (1991) had already emphasized the importance of monitoring and record-keeping during the transition process. They argued that this should take account of the whole child as physical, social, cognitive and emotional developmental needs are interdependent. It is hoped that schools will take account of this when special needs co-ordinators develop their special needs policies and practices in line with the Code of Practice.

Schools need to find effective ways of determining a child's skills on entry, gleaning this information not only from the linked nursery school but also from parents or any play groups or child minders who know the child.

The profile 'All About Me' (Wolfendale, 1987) developed in conjunction with the National Children's Bureau for parents to complete in a relaxed, informal way is an example of a strategy for collecting vital entry data on a child's language; play and learning; independence; physical development; health; habits; behaviour; moods and feelings.

Conclusion

This chapter has attempted to tease out some of the complex issues in relation to the impact of early intervention on children with social and behavioural difficulties. Whilst the provision of nursery education for all, would be laudable, it would in itself be insufficient to protect vulnerable children from the negative aspects of their later school career.

Based on the findings described above, I would argue that the following conditions need to be met to maximize the benefits of early intervention:

    (i)   A recognition that transition is an ongoing process which needs to be planned for, actively supported and followed through so that young children not only experience continuity and progression, but are also supported in dealing with learning challenges as and when they arrive;

    (ii)   Intervention and initiatives should not be dependent on the goodwill of an individual but should involve joint planning with all interested parties across institutions and should always include parents;

    (iii)   Social learning should be given the same value in schools as other aspects of the curriculum and young children's entry skills should be assessed in this area and their learning needs supported;

    (iv)   Strategies which involve the young child in active decision making situations with opportunities to work cooperatively with peers are likely to increase self-esteem and reduce difficult behaviour;

(v) Young children with social learning needs require structured learning environments where clear limits are set and positive recognition is given on a regular basis. Increasing a child's self-esteem and self-confidence through success reduces the need for that child to display unsocial behaviour.

During a debate in the House of Lords on the Education Bill (April 1993), Lady Warnock, whilst emphasizing the issues concerning good emotional development of children, reinforced the need for mainstream schools to have preventative systems in place before the stage is reached when special provision is needed.

In the debate Lord Swinfen also argued:

Resources given to children . . . may be expensive . . . but will be repaid a thousandfold as they become productive members of society when adult, rather than spending the rest of their lives in need of additional help.

It is still to be seen whether the government will respond to the clamour for more nursery provision and provide the necessary injection of capital which will enable local authorities to provide properly resourced and comprehensive nursery education for all pre-school children.

References

BARNETT, W.S. and ESCOBAR, C.M. (1990) 'The economic costs and benefits of early intervention, in MEISELS, S.J. and SHONKOFF, J.P. (Eds) *Handbook of Early Childhood Intervention*, Cambridge, Cambridge University Press.

BARRETT, M. and TREVITT, J. (1991) *Attachment Behaviour and the School Child: An Introduction to Educational Therapy*, London, Routledge.

BENNATHAN, M. (1993) *Taking Responsibility for Emotionally Damaged Children Young Minds*, June.

BROWN, S. and CLEAVE, S. (1991) *Four-year-olds in School: Quality Matters*, Slough, NFER.

CANTER, L. and CANTER, M. (1976) *Assertive Discipline: A Take Charge Approach for Today's Educator*, Santa Monica, CA, Lee Canter and Associates Inc.

CANTER, L. and CANTER, M. (1984) *Assertive Discipline: Resource Materials Workbook, Elementary K-6*, Santa Monica, CA, Lee Canter and Associates Inc.

CHAZAN, M. (1989) 'Bullying in the infant school', in TATTUM, D.P. and LANE, D.A. (Eds) *Bullying in Schools*, Stoke on Trent, Trentham Books Ltd.

CLARK, M. (1988) *Children Under 5: Educational Research and Evidence Final Report to the DES*, London, Gordan and Breach Science Publishers.

CLEAVE, S., JOWETT, S. and BATE, M. (1982) *And So to School: A Study of Continuity from Pre-school to Infant School*, Windsor, NFER Nelson.

CURTIS, A. (1986) *A Curriculum for the Pre-school Child*, Windsor, NFER Nelson.

DFE (1994) *Education Act 1993: Code of Practice on the Identification and Assessment of Special Educational Needs*, London DFE Publications Department.

DOUGLAS, J. (1989) *Behaviour Problems in Young Children*, London, Routledge.

Anne Rushton

ELTON, LORD (Chair) (1989) *Discipline in School: Report of the Committee of Inquiry*, London, HMSO.

FARRON, D.C. (1990) 'Effects of intervention with disadvantaged and disabled children: A decade view', in MEISELS, S.J. and SHOUKOFF, J.P. (Eds) *Handbook of Early Childhood Intervention*, Cambridge, Cambridge University Press.

FREDERICKSON, N. (1990) 'Teaching social skills to Children: Towards an integrated approach, *Education & Child Psychology*, **7**, 1, pp. 5–15.

GOLDING, J. and RUSH, D. (1986) 'Temper tantrums and other behaviour problems' in BATLER, N.R. and GOLDING, T. (Eds) *From Birth to Seven: A Study of the Health and Behaviour of Britain's Five Year Olds*, Oxford, Pergamon Press.

HALPERN, D.C. (1990) 'Community based early Intervention', in MEISELS, S.J. and SHOUKOFF, J.P. (Eds) *Handbook of Early Childhood Intervention*, Cambridge, Cambridge University Press.

HATTERSLEY, R. (1993) 'The lesson we must all learn to save our children', *Mail on Sunday*, 21 November.

HOWE, M.J.A. (1993) 'Home experience and the classroom discipline problems that can arise when needed skills are lacking in VARMA, VP (Ed) *Management of Behaviours in Schools*, Harlow, Longman.

HUTT, Y.S., TYLER, S., HUTT, C. and CHRISTOPHERSON, H. (1989) *Play, Exploration and Learning: A Natural History of the Pre-school*, London, Routledge.

JOWETT, S. and SYLVA, K. (1986) 'Does kind of pre-school matter?', *Educational Research*, **28**, 1, pp. 21–31.

MANNING and SLUCKIN (1984) 'The function of aggression in the pre-school and primary years', FRUDE, N., and GRULT, H. (Eds) *Disruptive Behaviour in School*, Chichester: Wiley.

REASON, R. (1991) 'Cooperating to learn and learning to cooperate: Primary school practices', in FREDERICKSON, N., HINTON, S., REASON, R. and WRIGHT, A. (Eds) *Developing Self Discipline*, University College London, Educational Psychology Publications.

RICHMAN, N., STEVENSON, J. and GRAHAM, P.J. (1982) *Pre school to School: A Behaviour Study*, London, Academic Press.

RUMBOLD, A. (Chair) (1990) *Starting with Quality* (Report of Committee of Inquiry into the Quality of the Educational Experience offered to 3 and 4 year-olds) London, HMSO.

RUTTER, M. (1985) 'Resilience in the face of adversity', *British Journal of Psychiatry*, **147**, pp. 598–611.

SCHWEINHART, L., BURRUETA-CLEMENT, Y., BARNETT, S., EPSTEIN, A. and WEIKART, D. (1985) 'Effects of the Perry Pre-school program on youth through age 19: A summary', *Topics in Early Childhood Special Education*, **5**, pp. 26–35.

SCHWEINHART, L., WEIKART, D. and LARNER, M. (1986a) 'Consequences of three pre-school curriculum models through age 15', *Early Childhood Research Quarterly*, **1**, pp. 15–45.

SCHWEINHART, L., WEIKART, D. and LARNER, M. (1986b) 'Child-initiated activities in early childhood programmes may help prevent delinquency', *Early Childhood Research Quarterly* pp. 303–12.

SYLVA, K., ROY, C. and PAINTER, M. (1980) *Childwatching at Playgroup and Nursery School*, London, Grant McIntyre.

TIZARD, B. (1975) *Early Childhood Education: A Review and Discussion of Research in Britain*, Slough, NFER/SSRC.

WERNER, E.E. (1990) 'Protective factors and individual resilience' in MEISELS, S.J. and SHORKOFF, J.P. (Eds) *Handbook of Early Childhood Intervention*, Cambridge, Cambridge University Press.

WOLFENDALE, (1987) 'The evaluation and revision of the "All about me" pre-school parent completed scales', *Early Child Development and Care*, **29**, pp. 473–558.

Chapter 8

Guidelines for Helping Children with Emotional and Behavioural Difficulties

Peter Farrell

Introduction

The Government has just published six separate circulars on 'Pupils with Problems' (DFE, 1994) four of which provide guidance on the following: pupil behaviour and discipline; emotional and behavioural difficulties; exclusions; and pupil referral units. Some of the guidance offered in them will be referred to at various stages throughout this chapter.

The idea of developing guidelines on how to help pupils with emotional and behavioural difficulties is not new. Indeed the DFE Circular on *Pupil Behaviour and Discipline* reminds all schools of the need to develop whole school behaviour policies; it offers guidance on how these should be developed and on their possible contents. Many special schools for pupils with severe learning difficulties and emotional and behavioural problems have also developed consistent handling strategies for managing individual pupils which are informed by their discipline policy. Several books and in-service materials also contain guidelines for teachers on various aspects of classroom management (see, for example, Canter and Canter, 1992; Chisholm *et al.*, 1986; Hart and Mongon, 1989; Wheldall and Merrett, 1990a and b; Charlton and David, 1993). The DFE circulars contain guidance on how schools should apply Government legislation, as does the Department of Health's Guidelines on permissable forms of control, (DOH, 1993). The latter will be referred to in some detail later in this chapter. Finally, all local authorities produce guidelines on child protection procedures.

In this chapter it is not the intention to replace or upstage existing guidelines. On the contrary the aim is to draw from existing guidelines so as to provide suggestions for good practice in schools and for support services. These should be helpful to practitioners who are thinking of developing or updating their own guidelines.

Much of the contents of this chapter may appear at first sight to be common sense and to be stating the obvious. This accusation could also be levelled at the DFE circulars. But common sense is not always easy to apply! We can all think of times when we have behaved inappropriately and have made matters worse either professionally as teachers or in our personal life. How many of us can honestly say that we have treated pupils fairly at all times, have never publicly humiliated a pupil, sworn at the neighbour's dog or even at the neighbour! With hindsight 'common sense' would tell us that we had acted stupidly and we may privately or even publicly express regret. However, even with the benefit of hindsight and prolonged reflection, we may still behave the same way again on another occasion. We, like our pupils, are only human and can act inappropriately without thinking things through. Therefore, although these guidelines, may appear to be common sense, they are an attempt to help practitioners to behave in a fair, rational and planned way when helping pupils with emotional and behaviour problems and so reduce the chance that we may act hastily and without thinking.

Formal written guidelines are often quite detailed and can make the whole process of managing pupils with challenging behaviour look rather mechanical and dispassionate. It is not easy to put into words the heat, feelings and emotion that can be generated in a crisis that may be felt by staff and pupils alike. Events move extremely quickly in a crisis and it is a lot to ask of staff to be calm and have all the relevant guidelines at their finger tips. Therefore guidelines are not, and could never be, the whole answer. Although they should inform good practice for the majority of the time, there will always be occasions when the procedures to follow when an incident occurs may not be adhered to. Hopefully, the consequences of ignoring or forgetting guidelines will not always be catastrophic but this depends on the nature of the guidelines which have not been followed. Some guidelines are enshrined in law and ignoring them can have serious consequences.

There are two sets of guidelines which follow, one aimed at headteachers and senior managers in schools and one for class teachers and other 'front line' staff. There is an obvious overlap between the guidelines and it is important for teachers and support services to be familiar with both of them. The guidelines for headteachers and senior managers have been drawn from research and practice on effective schools, effective ways of managing change and the psychology of organizations. The guidelines for class teachers have been drawn from research and practice on classroom management and from the Department of Health's guidance which relates to the Children Act, DOH (1993).

Guidelines for Headteachers and Senior Managers

Underpinning the following guidelines is the need for schools to create a positive ethos. The DFE Circular on *Pupil Behaviour and Discipline* emphasizes the role of the governing body in this respect. Ethos is a word which is often used but hard to define. Rutter *et al.* (1979) used the term to distinguish between schools with a positive ethos which were associated with good standards of behaviour and low truancy rates from schools with a negative ethos where the opposite was the case. Schools with a positive ethos tend to have a general atmosphere and policies which successfully encourage pupils and parents to feel welcome in the school and where rewards rather than punishments are used to encourage learning and good behaviour. The following guidelines should help schools to develop a positive ethos although the uniqueness of each school means that the factors in one school which contribute towards a positive ethos may be different from another.

(i)   Develop, monitor and review whole school policies on helping pupils with emotional and behavioural problems

The DFE Circular on *Pupils with Problems* urges schools to produce whole school behaviour policies and provides guidance on how these should be developed. It suggests that the policy should contain the following features:

- it should be based on a clear and defensible set of principles and values;
- mutual respect is useful starting point;
- the policy should encourage good behaviour rather than simply punish bad behaviour;
- the policy should be specific to the school;
- rules should be kept to a minimum;
- the reasons for each rule should be obvious; and
- wherever possible rules should be expressed in positive constructive terms.

It also suggests the stages which schools might go through when developing their policy. These stress the need for all staff to be involved and for parents and pupils to be consulted. This 'bottom up' approach, if successfully applied, will take time but should result in the policy being successfully implemented. However it is important for it to be regularly monitored and reviewed.

(ii) Create an atmosphere which encourages openness in discussions between classteachers and senior managers

It is in the nature of the job that headteachers and senior managers are experienced teachers, better paid than class teachers and in a position of power over their junior colleagues. It is not uncommon for hard pressed classteachers to feel resentful about what they may perceive to be the 'protected' and 'less pressurized' role of the senior manager. Remarks such as 'it's all very well for them to tell me what to do but how often do they have to take a class of thirty unruly pupils' are not unknown. Managers more often than not deal with the consequences of misbehaviour, (for example, when the child is sent to the headteacher to explain his/her misbehaviour) and not with the behaviour itself. Therefore, underpinning these guidelines is the need for senior managers to be sensitive to criticisms of this sort and to do everything possible to counteract them.

If a member of staff is experiencing problems managing a class or an individual pupil, he/she should feel able to discuss the situation openly with a senior member of staff. Too often classteachers have soldiered on alone for fear of being made to feel a failure if they discuss their problems with others. It is not necessarily a sign of weakness if a teacher experiences discipline problems and indeed *all* teachers, even those who are promoted to senior positions, will have experienced difficulties at the start of their career. It is therefore vital for senior managers to support their staff who are having problems.

Special Educational Needs Coordinators (SENCOs) will have an important role in discussing discipline problems with staff and in offering guidance and support. They and other members of the senior management team need to make themselves available to offer help and to be proactive in supporting staff who have hitherto not asked for it. This role clearly demands a high degree of sensitivity and good interpersonal skills.

(iii) Have clearly defined roles for staff

Staff should know who has responsibility for all aspects of helping pupils who have emotional and behavioural problems. This could include responsibility for dealing with outside agencies, for contacting parents, for dealing with crises. Clearly the larger the school the more important it is for these staff roles to be made clear. SENCOs will have a pivotal role in ensuring that this takes place.

(iv) Establish teams of staff who work well together

Thomas (1992) has stressed the value and importance of effective classroom teamwork. For some time primary schools have employed a team teaching approach. In recent years there has also been a trend for support teachers to work with pupils with special needs in mainstream classes rather than withdrawing them to another room. Effective teamwork can dramatically reduce the incidence of classroom disruption. It is therefore vital for senior staff to as far as possible establish teams which work well together. In secondary schools this also applies to departmental teams.

(v) Establish a mechanism whereby regular meetings can be held to plan and review programmes for individuals who are causing concern

Whenever a school is concerned about a child's behaviour it is important to develop a consistent handling strategy to plan a programme of intervention. Such a policy should be planned at a meeting of relevant staff and outside agencies, the parents and if possible the pupil. Regular meetings should then be held to monitor and review the programme.

(vi) Develop good working relationships with other agencies

All schools have access to education welfare and educational psychology services. Many LEAs also have support services for pupils with learning, behaviour, physical and sensory difficulties. Furthermore, staff from health and social services have regular contact with schools. It is vitally important for senior staff to get to know the agencies which are available to support the school and to become familiar with their brochures. These services can offer advice to SENCOs on how to implement the first three stages of assessment outlined in the Code of Practice and educational psychologists and staff from the behavioural support service should be able to offer general advice on individuals and groups of pupils. They also have a detailed knowledge of the range of SEN provision that is available in the LEA.

Due to ongoing financial constraints within which LEAs work and to the implementation of LMS the role and future of many support services is uncertain. Smith and Thomas (1993) describe the situation as being 'ad hoc and piecemeal'. There is insufficient space in this chapter to discuss the issues in detail. However, in order for schools to work as effectively as possible with their support services it is important for them to be clear about the kind of support they would like to receive. The services may not have the time, expertise or resources to provide this level of support but it helps if they know what schools would like!

(vii) Ensure that there are sufficient opportunities for staff development and training

The implementation of the 1993 Education Act and the Code of Practice together with the publication of the DFE Circulars highlights the continued and vital need for staff to receive in-service training in special needs and particularly in the area of children with emotional and behavioural difficulties. Senior staff should support in-service training by making sure that the school's inservice budget is sufficient to cover the need, by drawing on the expertise of support services and by liaising with their local institute of higher education.

Peter Farrell

Guidelines for Teachers

These are divided into three sections. The first covers general points, the second discusses factors to consider when setting up a specific programme and the third focuses on the Department of Health's guidelines on permissable forms of control which relate to the provisions of the Children Act.

General Points

(i) At all times pupils should be engaged in useful activities which are of interest to them and at their ability level

This is the sort of guideline which is easy to write and almost impossible to implement. Taken literally, to implement this guideline each classteacher, no matter how large the class, should know the precise ability level of all the pupils in all areas of the curriculum and organize the lessons such that each pupil is working at his/her assessed level on a curriculum area in which they are interested throughout the day. With thirty or more pupils in a class this is extremely difficult if not impossible to do. However, that does not mean that it is not worthwhile striving to achieve this aim. The research on classroom management and the incidence of behaviour problems in classrooms shows firstly, that the more involved and interested pupils are in their work, the less likelihood there is of behaviour problems occurring and secondly, that the best way to manage behaviour problems is to prevent them occurring in the first place (see Wheldall and Merrett, 1990a and 1990b for a more thorough discussion of the issues). This guideline, therefore, represents a crucial preventative strategy which all teachers should aim to achieve. When faced with a pupil or group of pupils who are misbehaving an essential first step is to see if this guideline is being adhered to.

(ii) Teachers should like and respect the pupils

If teachers like their pupils there is a much greater chance that behaviour problems can be dealt with amicably. However it would be amazing if teachers liked *all* their pupils *all* the time. Therefore if there is antipathy, it is important to acknowledge this and try to overcome these feelings by talking them through with a colleague. In extreme circumstances a teacher may be frightened of a pupil and again it is better to acknowledge this fear and talk it over rather than try to intervene with the pupil without seeking help.

(iii) When there is a problem seek support from colleagues and senior staff

When faced with a pupil or class whose behaviour is difficult to manage it is important not to go it alone but to seek help and support from colleagues. It is important that the act of seeking help is not seen as an admission of failure and therefore all staff should be open about problems they have so that a climate of honesty and respect for others' strengths and needs is established.

(iv) Follow school and LEA policies

Teachers should study and implement the school's policies on behaviour and special needs and should take an active part in rewriting and improving them as and when necessary.

(v) Negotiate a few class rules with the pupils and stick to them

This is one of the keys to successful classroom management. Rules should be phased positively. 'Always arrive on time for lessons' is better then 'Don't be late for lessons'. If at all possible rules should be negotiated with the class at the start of the term and should be visible for all to see.

(vi) Be calm

This is another guideline which is easy to write but not always easy to implement. However, its importance cannot be overstressed. Teachers who are calm are more likely to be in control of themselves and the situation. Losing control may result in teachers saying or doing things they may regret and result in a loss of respect from the pupils. We frequently blame pupils for losing control if they get into an argument or a fight and it is therefore important for teachers not to lay themselves open to the same accusation.

(vii) Be consistent

Again this is not always easy to do. However, research on pupils' perceptions of teaching shows that being fair and consistent is rated the most highly as being the factor which they value most from their teachers. The often used phrase 'don't promise or threaten anything you can't deliver' is extremely relevant in this context.

(viii) Rewards work better than punishments

Again this is a key finding from all research on classroom management, (see for example, O'Leary and O'Leary, 1977; Rutter *et al.*, 1979; Wheldall and Merrett, 1990a and 1990b). Rewards help to promote a positive ethos in the school and are likely to contribute to building a positive relationship between teacher and pupils. It is therefore important for teachers to get to know their pupils well so that they can establish which rewards work best for them. Pupils have complex and developing personalities and rewards which work for one child may not work for another. In general, as pupils get older, the range of rewards which may work becomes more complex. Pupils in infant schools will often find a star chart rewarding and will enjoy being praised in front of the whole class. In secondary schools the same 'rewards' would be positively unrewarding for many pupils.

Guidelines for Setting Up a Specific Programme

So far we have looked at general guidelines to follow which have focused on preventing emotional and behavioural problems from occurring as well as at some general strategies for intervention. However there are times when teachers, possibly in consultation with other professionals, will develop a specific strategy to deal with a problem. The following guidelines refer to points which should be considered when setting up such a programme. They apply equally to setting up a programme for an individual pupil or to groups, for example, the whole class.

(i)   Involve everybody in planning the intervention

This is particularly important when planning a programme for an individual pupil. 'Everybody' means the teachers who know the pupil best, outside agencies, the parents and the pupil. The aim should be to arrive at a position where everybody agrees about the nature of the problem, the causes and what to do about it. This may not be easy to achieve but as a starting point it is important for everyone to get together to discuss the problem so that the risk of someone feeling excluded is reduced and there is a greater chance that everybody will cooperate with the programme. Such meetings are normally held when setting up a behavioural contract (see McNamara, 1987). These meetings need to be handled carefully as feelings may be running high, particularly if the people involved have different views about the extent and/or cause of the problem. For example, parents may think that their child's behaviour problems are caused by poor teaching or by other pupils picking on the child. The school may see things very differently. Issues such as where such meetings should be held and who chairs them are also important. They should not be seen as an opportunity for one party to blame the other. Parents in particular should not be made to feel overawed by the occasion and should take part in the discussion as equal partners.

(ii)   Observe the behaviours carefully

It may well be that having gathered everybody together and discussed the situation, that people are still unclear as to the extent or cause of the problem. It is therefore important to observe the behaviour carefully paying particular attention to the following factors.

The setting: where and what time of day does the behaviour occur, for example, the classroom, during PE, during afternoon break.

The antecedents: what happens immediately before the behaviour takes place, for example, the school bell rings, the teacher leaves the classroom.

The behaviour itself: what precisely happens; described in observable terms.

The consequences: what happens immediately after the behaviour, for example, how does the teacher react, what do the pupils do. What effect does all this have on the pupil.

This kind of analysis will be familiar to people who have been involved in planning traditional behaviour modification programmes. It has been advocated by Westmacot and Cameron (1981), Wheldall and Merrett (1990a and 1990b) and many others including the new Draft Circular referred to earlier. Whatever one's views about the effectiveness of behavioural approaches, there is no doubt that a detailed analysis of the setting conditions, antecedents, behaviours and consequences can help us to understand a great deal about the nature of our behaviour and how to change it.

(iii)   Be explicit about the behaviour to change and realistic about when this could be achieved

Don't be too ambitious; make sure everybody, especially the pupil, knows precisely what the programme is hoping to achieve and has agreed about it. When trying to change behaviour it is better to set modest targets which could be reached in a relatively short space of time for example, two weeks.

(iv)   Make intervention strategies explicit

These should be clear to everybody and include information on who should do what when undesirable behaviour occurs, what rewards will be used, how will the programme be monitored, when will it be reviewed and by whom and what support is required. The strategy should be consistently applied; in general desirable behaviour should be rewarded and inappropriate behaviour dealt with in an ethically acceptable manner which does not effect relationships with the pupil(s).

Peter Farrell

The Department of Health's Guidance

No matter how good a school's preventative strategies are, how well a setting is managed, how well resourced and how good the morale of the staff, we still may need to use strategies which involve restricting children's liberty, holding or restraining them. These strategies are potentially open to abuse. In order to advise staff on these matters the Department of Health has issued a Circular entitled *Guidance on Permissable Forms of Control in Children's Residential Care* (DOH, 1993). The guidance is derived from and builds on volume 4 of the Children Act Guidance and Regulations. The DFE has sent it to all independent schools catering for children with SEN, to all non-maintained special schools and 'endorses the advice and guidance offered'. Although the guidance and covering letter do not explicitly say so, one can reasonably assume that it applies to all schools and indeed it is referred to in the recent Circular on *Children with Emotional and Behavioural Difficulties*, referred to above.

The guidance focuses on strategies to help pupils whose behaviour is extremely violent and aggressive where people or property may be damaged. Although they do no state this, the impression is that the DOH believes these kinds of behaviours would not normally be found in mainstream schools. This might explain the limited circulation of the guidance.

The decision to make provisions in the Children Act and produce guidelines on permissable forms of control arose from adverse publicity on the management of children with behaviour problems, notably that which led to the 'Pin Down' enquiry into methods that were used to control children's behaviour in residential settings in Staffordshire. Hence it is important to remember that although these guidelines apply to all professionals who work with children in any setting, they arose out of unacceptable practices employed by residential workers in children's homes.

The main focus of the guidelines is on acceptable and effective techniques to deal with violent and aggressive behaviour. The key point is that techniques such as *physical restraint* or those which are designed to *restrict liberty* can only be used if there is a risk that the child will damage himself/herself, other people or property. In no other circumstances should children's liberty be restricted or physical restraint used.

The guidelines then proceed to discuss alternative methods of using 'physical presence' and 'holding' before describing how physical restraint should be applied when the child is in danger of injuring him/herself or property and the implications of the regulations on the restriction of liberty.

(i)   Use of physical presence

This can be used to reinforce the staff's authority and concern. Staff may stand in the way of a pupil who is trying to run out of class or place a hand on his/her arm. It should be used 'in the context of trying to engage the child in discussion about the significance and implications of his behaviour' (p. 16). If the child physically resists, another technique will be needed.

(ii)   Holding

The DOH guidelines distinguish between 'holding' and 'physical restraint', or try to. In general, holding is permissable as it involves less force and therefore can be used even if there is no risk of the child damaging him/ herself, others or property. The distinction between the two techniques is not easy to define. The guidelines state that the main factor separating one from the other is 'the manner of intervention and the **degree of force applied**. Physical restraint uses the degree of force necessary to *prevent* a child harming himself or others or property. Holding would *discourage* but in itself would not prevent such an action' (p. 16–17).

The guidelines suggest that holding may be an appropriate technique to use when guiding a child away from a confrontation with another pupil or when insisting on holding a child's hand to cross a road.

When applying the holding technique the member of staff should:

(a)   know the child and explain why holding is being used;
(b)   use another method if the child forcibly resists in consultation with other staff;
(c)   ensure that sexual expectations or feelings are not been aroused.

(iii)   Physical restraint

As already stated, physical restraint can only be used if the child's behaviour may damage him/herself or property. This technique may be used to prevent a child from attacking someone or from smashing furniture or if he/she is threatening to run out of the building with the suspected intention of damaging others or property. In 1993 a primary school teacher clearly flouted this aspect of the guidelines by placing sticking plaster over the mouths of her pupils to prevent them from speaking. This was an unacceptable use of physical restraint as in no way were the children in danger of damaging people or property by making a noise!

When using physical restraint staff should:

(a)   give a warning that physical restraint will be used;
(b)   use the 'minimum' force necessary;
(c)   ensure other staff are present;
(d)   gradually withdraw the restraint to allow child to regain self-control;
(e)   record the action taken;

(f) discuss the incident with the line manager;

(g) discuss the incident with the child involved.

The above suggestions, though helpful, may in practice be extremely difficult to apply. It is likely that a technique such as physical restraint will be needed when the situation is tense and charged with emotion. In this atmosphere staff have to make snap judgments and it may not be possible, or even desirable, to wait until another member of staff is present as by the time this happens, someone might have been hurt or property damaged.

(iv) Restriction of liberty

Under section 25 of the Children Act children's liberty can only be restricted if they are placed in a community home with secure accommodation approved by the Secretary of State. Such children are likely to have committed criminal offences and/or to have a record of persistent absconding and whilst absconding are likely to suffer 'significant harm'. In no other circumstances is it permissable to forcibly restrict a child's liberty.

For all but the tiny minority of children who are placed in secure units it is therefore illegal to lock a child in a room even for a very short period of time. This practice, often referred to as 'time out', has been relatively common in day and residential schools for children with challenging behaviour and emotional and behaviour difficulties and is now clearly illegal. The DOH guidelines are ambiguous about measures to restrict children's liberty which fall short of locking a child in a room, for example, shutting a child in a room with a member of staff standing on the other side of the door to prevent an escape. The legality of such measures will 'ultimately be determined by the courts'. It suggests that such action may on occasions be necessary to prevent injury or damage to people or property and urges local authorities to seek legal advice when formulating their guidance to staff.

Physical restraint, using the guidelines summarized above, should only be used to restrict a child's liberty if failure to do so may result in injury to people or property. If there is no reason to believe that this will occur, then other methods short of using physical restraint must be used.

The law on the restriction of liberty enshrined in the Children Act has caused some problems for staff who are involved teaching and caring for children with severe challenging behaviour (Jones, personal communication; Wolkind, 1993). Techniques such as time out have proved to be effective when used carefully with the agreement of all parties. Many residential establishments which cater for children with serious emotional and behavioural problems have had to rethink their strategies and guidelines to take account of the provisions of the Act.

In addition to the sections, summarized above, the DOH guidelines also refer to the need for establishments to have a positive ethos and to base their management strategies on using rewards rather than punishments. In this respect they are similar to the recent DFE circulars. The DOH guidelines also stress the need for staff to be adequately trained, a point which is conspicuously absent from the DFE Circulars.

Conclusion

As mentioned in the introduction, it has not been the aim of this chapter to replace or upstage existing guidelines. The intention has been to raise key points on the development of guidelines on a range of issues related to the effective management of children with emotional and behavioural difficulties. These should be helpful to staff who wish to develop, revise and improve their own guidelines. The specific nature of any school's set of guidelines should inevitably reflect the unique needs of the school.

References

CANTER, L. and CANTER, M. (1992) *Assertive Discipline: Positive Management for Today's Classrooms*, Bristol, Behaviour Management Ltd.

CHARLTON, T. and DAVID, K. (1993) *Managing Misbehaviour in Schools* (2nd edn) London, Routledge.

CHISHOLM, B., KEARNEY, D., KNIGHT, G. LITTLE, H., MORRIS, S. and TWEDDLE, D. (1986) *Preventative Approaches to Disruption*, London, Macmillan Education.

DFE (1993) *Pupils with Problems*, Draft Circulars, London, Department for Education Publications Department.

DOH (1993) *Guidance on Permissable Forms of Control in Children's Residential Care*, London, Department of Health Publications Unit.

HART, S. and MONGON, D. (1989) *Improving Classroom Behaviour: New Directions for Teachers and Pupils*, London, Cassell.

JONES, M. (personal communication) 'Implications of the Children Act for the education and care of children whose special needs are compounded by severe challenging behaviour'.

McNAMARA, E. (1987) 'Behavioural contracting with secondary aged pupils', *Educational Psychology in Practice*, **2**, 4, pp. 21–6.

O'LEARY, K.D. and O'LEARY, S.G. (1977) *Classroom Management: The Successful use of Behaviour Modification, Second Edition*, Oxford, Pergamon Press.

RUTTER, M., MAUGHAN, B., MORTIMORE, P. and OUSTON, J. (1979) *Fifteen Thousand Hours: Secondary Schools and their Effects on Children*, London, Open Books.

SMITH, A. and THOMAS, J. (1993) 'The psychological support of pupils with emotional and behavioural difficulties', *Support for Learning*, **8**, 3, pp. 104–6.

Tameside MBC (1993) *WRAP*, Manchester, Tameside Metropolitan Borough Education Department.

THOMAS, G. (1992) *Effective Classroom Teamwork: Support or Consultation*, London, Routledge.

WESTMACOT, S. and CAMERON, R.J. (1981) *Behaviour Can Change*, London, Macmillan Education.

WHELDALL, K. and MERRETT, F. (1990a) *Positive Teaching in the Secondary School*, London, Paul Chapman Publishing.

WHELDALL, K. and MERRETT, F. (1990b) *Positive Teaching in the Primary School*, London, Paul Chapman Publishing.

WOLKIND, S. (1993) 'The Children Act: A cynical view from an ivory tower', *Association of Child Psychology and Psychiatry Review and Newsletter*, **15**, 1, pp. 40–1.

Chapter 9

A Whole School Approach to the Management of Pupil Behaviour

Andy Samson and Georgina Hart

Introduction

When the Elton Report was published in 1989 it was widely agreed that it contained a comprehensive and up-to-date analysis of the extent of problem behaviour in schools. Large-scale violence in the classroom was not seen to be a major problem. What was a problem, however, was the continuously disruptive behaviour of many pupils. 'Beaten down — not beaten up' was the message it gave back to all who were involved in education.

One of its recommendations was that local education authorities should provide specialist help in order to produce strategies that would prove effective for all schools. Tameside Education Authority appointed their own multidisciplinary project team to undertake this work. Thus began our work as the Tameside Elton Project.

In this chapter we provide an outline of the system we developed to work with schools and this is followed by an example of how this was put into practice to help one school develop its policy on bullying.

Developing a Model of Working

We were fortunate in that we were given time at the beginning of the project to consider how best we might benefit the schools in our area. Consequently from the outset we were not faced with having to don crime buster equipment and immediately prove our worth. Instead we were able to consider our options and to ask ourselves pertinent questions, namely:

- What do the schools want?
- Who do we ask?
- How do we deliver?

In the time we had available we visited a large number of schools collecting information about what they felt would be of most use to them. From these

Figure 9.1: Four stages of the Elton team's input with schools

Teachers Pupils Non-teachers Parents	**Stage 1**	**Information Collection**
Documentation Staff meetings Tutorial time Assemblies Newsletters Governors' meetings	**Feedback and identification of priorities**	**Stage 2**
INSET Rewards Sanctions Bullying Code of conduct Lunchtime organization	**Stage 3**	**Input and initiatives**
Are there changes in place? Are there changes in behaviour?	**Evaluation**	**Stage 4**

informal interviews with headteachers, teachers and non-teaching staff came two very crucial points.

First, the circumstance of each school, catchment area, experience of the staff and building make each school unique. Second, schools wanted an involvement which produced a practical outcome specifically relevant to each of them.

Armed with this information, we developed a model (see figure 9.1) which we felt could be adapted by each school in the Authority. This model was divided into four stages and proved very successful in providing a structure to enable the needs of individual schools to be met.

Stage 1 was an information gathering stage, much of which was obtained with the use of questionnaires, interviews and observation.

We administered questionnaires as follows:

Figure 9.2: Gathering information across Tameside schools

Schools

Number of schools receiving a full input from the Elton team	22
Number of schools having other involvement, for example, INSET	14

Pupils

Number of pupils completing questionnaires	2,871
Number of pupils interviewed by Elton team	1,240

Teachers

Number of teachers completing questionnaires	483
Number of teachers interviewed by Elton team	371

Non-teachers (Welfare Assistants, Secretaries, Caretakers)

Number of non-teachers interviewed by Elton team	198

Parents

Number of parents completing questionnaires	2,182
Highest questionnaire % returned rate	92%
Lowest questionnaire % returned rate	52%
Number of parents interviewed	230
Number of newsletters sent to parents	7,550

To pupils

(a) In primary schools to the top two years;

(b) In secondary schools to one class per year group.

We also interviewed a cross-section of pupils from all age groups.

To staff

We gave every member of staff a questionnaire usually at staff meetings when they could be completed and returned immediately. Putting questionnaires in staff pigeon holes was quickly discarded as the number of returns was low.

In the later part of the project we interviewed all teaching staff.

To parents

We issued questionnaires in envelopes to all the parents. This produced an average return of 75 per cent.

We interviewed a random sample of parents.

Non-teaching staff

We interviewed secretaries, caretakers and lunchtime organizers.

Figure 9.2 illustrates how many people were involved in this process.

At this point, it is important to note that we found the information gathering stage crucial. Any school wishing to adopt this model will find a wealth of information comes from this stage which can be used for future developments.

Stage 2 was the feedback which led to the identification of areas for future action. All staff received the results of the survey in booklet form. This booklet provided the basis for a staff meeting where areas for development were identified by staff and the team. Recommendations for action were made by the team. These, however were fluid and open to negotiation.

In all the schools with which we worked this identification of areas for development was made easy by the survey results which highlighted those areas where development work was necessary. After the feedback all schools agreed that it would be sensible to work on one area before moving onto the next rather than tackle two issues simultaneously. It was also therefore a time of forward planning and timetabling so that staff did not feel overburdened. For example, schools would decide to redesign a Code of Conduct before moving on to look at rewards and sanctions.

Pupils received a feedback via assemblies and tutor periods and were encouraged to contribute their ideas with regard to the way forward.

Parents received feedback through a newsletter which informed them of results and invited comment on future developments that would be taking place. Many schools continued to send out newsletters as new procedures were put into place. One important outcome for both us and the schools was the high level of support which parents showed towards their children's schools and teachers. 'More information please' was a standard cry from parents. Schools found they could act upon this request effectively by introducing regular newsletters.

Governors were also involved and survey results were introduced at governors meetings and discussed thoroughly. Future developments were speedily endorsed by governors with such information readily to hand.

Stage 3 was the input of new initiatives.

One of the most valuable aspects of the information survey was the speed and effectiveness with which new initiatives could be introduced into the school. The consultation of teachers, parents and pupils had meant that everyone was aware of what was going on and therefore had an investment in the success of the new developments. For example, a new code of conduct had been widely discussed and agreed upon before publication. This ensured its acceptance by all concerned. It is important to note that schools with which we worked also kept non-teaching staff fully informed and included them in the implementation of new initiatives.

Stage 4 was the evaluation of the effectiveness of the new initiatives. This was and is ongoing. No new development was introduced as 'tablets of stone' and a built-in appraisal of the success of the initiative is intended as part of the process.

Schools were looking to see if any changes resulted from the initiative. If this was not the case what further changes were needed to be made for it to become effective. For example if, as in the case of an excellent reward system we evaluated for a school, it appeared that certain rewards were much easier to attain than others (which caused confusion for the pupils), it was easy to put right once the problem had been identified.

One important aspect of a whole school survey is that it also identifies what is working well. It was important to the schools and to us and served as a reminder that schools are hard working places and that teachers are trying hard to keep pace with the constant changes that are being heaped upon them.

General Points Across Schools

We became aware that schools recognized above all the need for CONSIST-ENCY. This was what schools strove to achieve. It is widely recognized by all educationalists that consistency in delivering the curriculum is of benefit to all involved in school life. It can be argued that it is a great deal more difficult to apply this consistency of approach to behavioural issues if only because human beings do not behave consistently. None the less the key for schools embarking on a behaviour policy is consistency of approach to all aspects of school life.

With this in mind the following areas were identified by schools as being the main points which needed to be addressed if they were to produce an effective policy on behaviour.

   (i)   Whole School Policy;
   (ii)   Code of Conduct;
   (iii)   Effective Rewards;
   (iv)   Effective Sanctions;
   (v)   Effective Classroom Management;
   (vi)   Tackling Individual Behaviour Problems;
   (vii)   Effective Bullying Policy;
   (viii)   Lunchtime/Playtime Behaviour;
   (ix)   Parental Links;
   (x)   Promoting Good Attendance.

Developing a Whole School Policy on Bullying

In this chapter we have given a brief outline of how we worked with schools in assisting them to produce behaviour policies. As an example of how the Elton team worked with schools we now include below an account of how one school produced a Bullying Policy. This example has been chosen because the subject is one of concern to all schools.

In all the schools that we worked with in Tameside bullying was identi-fied by both pupils and parents as causing problems. Between 40 and 60 per cent of the pupils questioned felt that they had been bullied at some time since starting school. This percentage was reflected in the parents' questionnaires when they were asked if they were worried about their children being bullied.

Again between 40 and 60 per cent replied 'Yes'! All schools took this information seriously and some immediately took action and set about the process of producing written policies that were aimed at preventing bullying. This part of the chapter will describe that process and how it was applied in a Community High School in Tameside.

The school first of all looked at the aims of a bullying policy? They agreed that it should aim to:

- prevent bullying;
- give guidelines for dealing with bullying if it occurs;
- become an integral part of the school discipline policy;
- become part of the PSE policy.

The school then decided that their policy should contain:

- ways of raising awareness about what is bullying;
- ways of encouraging children to talk about bullying;
- how 'difficult' areas of the school can be supervised;
- guidelines for investigating bullying incidents;
- guidelines for dealing with victims, witnesses and bullies.

The school staff gave several reasons for producing a Bullying Policy. Among these were:

- We need to identify what our pupils mean by bullying;
- We need to know how to deal with bullies and victims;
- We need to consider how we should involve parents when dealing with cases of bullying;
- We need to find out when and where bullying is taking place;
- We should help our pupils learn how to cope with bullying situations.

The headteacher also stated that 'one case of bullying is one case too many'.

In general all staff agreed that perhaps the most important reason was that the school wanted their pupils to be happy and feel secure.

Figure 9.3 illustrates the action plan which illustrates how the bullying policy was put into practice.

At the conclusion of the project we asked the school to let us know what they felt were the benefits of having a written policy on dealing with bullying. The responses we received were as follows:

- It has helped to raise awareness amongst pupils and encouraged victims of bullying to seek help;
- It has improved relationships with parents who now have confidence that the school will deal with incidents of bullying;

Figure 9.3:   How the policy was put into practice

HOW?	ACTION	WHY?
Survey of pupils, teachers, non-teaching staff and parents. Establish a working party	Step 1 Acknowledge that bullying takes place.	This establishes the extent of the problem and the view of the various groups. It also identifies problem areas.
By the working party using the survey information or using an INSET day.	Step 2 Define bullying.	Establishes exactly what is meant by bullying and prevents misunderstandings.
Staff guidelines, pupil guidelines and non-teaching staff guidelines. Parental information.	Step 3 Develop consistent systems/approaches /strategies to help individuals deal with incidents.	Supports staff and pupils. Reassures parents. Ensures staff are not isolated when dealing with incidents.
Working party /small task groups.	Step 4 Write a school policy.	Reassure both parents and pupils that the school is doing something about bullying.
Assemblies, form periods. Pupil handbook/diary. Parents letter, newsletter, staff handbook. School brochure.	Step 5 Communicate the school policy to everyone.	To ensure confidence in that all incidents of bullying will be dealt with. Ensure changes take place. Everyone clear as to procedures/guidelines.
Extra supervision. Playground duties, supervision of corridors, toilets etc. Review of lunchtime supervision. School bus supervision.	Step 6 Make organizational changes.	Helps prevent bullying and deals with the problem areas identified in the survey.
Tutor periods, parents letter. Staff/pastoral meetings.	Step 7 Evaluation.	Do any changes that need to be made.

N.B. In step 2 the school involved the pupils by holding workshops. This information from the pupils was used when writing the pupil guidelines.

- The guidelines have given staff confidence in dealing with bullying incidents;
- It has reduced incidents of bullying to a minimum.

Conclusion

We feel that our work in Tameside shows that it is possible for an outside team to work effectively in schools. It was clear that staff, parents and pupils were all keen to improve behaviour in schools and welcomed our involvement. By working closely with all parties concerned we found it possible to identify specific areas of concern and produce whole school strategies for modifying pupil behaviour.

Chapter 10

Exclusion: Failed Children or Systems Failure?

Vanessa Parffrey

Political and Legislative Background

The 1981 Education Act in Britain offered special education a new spirit and a new vision. It was one that promoted inclusiveness — of a common entitlement for all children to have their intellectual, physical, emotional and behavioural needs met, and wherever possible, within the mainstream classroom. Difference was to be celebrated and embraced, schools worked cooperatively to meet these needs, a sense of shared responsibility for all children predominated. Integration was the key word.

During the 1980s, this positive spirit towards children who were different, and even difficult, developed. The 1986 Education Act and the Elton Report (1989) focused particularly on the problems of discipline in our schools. Both reiterated the spirit of integration and common responsibility and both promoted the need for positive, preventative approaches in order to reduce the disruption and the development of clear behavioural policies in our schools.

There were children, of course, who were still not responding to this clarity, and provision for those excluded from school was to be found either on home tuition, or a small unit might be provided for the few who were excluded.

In an article on the inception and rationale of one such unit (Parffrey, 1990) I end by fearing that greater provision of units may result in greater demand for the provision, i.e. a greater number of exclusions, but conclude that it is a question of purpose. That is, if the main purpose is to return the children back to mainstream school or, with those in their last year, work in partnership with the 'source' schools, then maybe such a unit is justified. If, however, it merely allows the schools to abdicate responsibility for these children, and the school plays no further part in their education, then the units may well have a detrimental effect. I conclude that in the case of exclusion units 'small may very well be beautiful'. That is, ideally, such units should be continually trying to work themselves out of a job.

Then came the 1988 Education Act. Gone was the spirit of cooperation, and shared responsibility. Rather, the Act purposely thrust schools into the market place for 'buying' by parents. Schools, with their devolved budgets, were set against each other in direct competition. The imposition of a National Curriculum and national testing, meant that schools' results could be made available for public scrutiny and comparison. Suddenly — and it *was* very sudden — schools were being judged and compared on criteria that hitherto had been perceived to be but only *one* of their tasks. That is that academic attainment, alone, was the sole indicator of performance. A school's effectiveness in the many other areas deemed relevant and part of a child's 'education', was, in one swoop, ignored. The pastoral care and teaching of children with differences — particularly behavioural and emotional difficulties — was one of these curriculum casualties.

The new anxieties over image and performance, I suggest, put back the clock. The spirit in our schools regressed to an almost Victorian ethos — of intolerance and impatience towards difference and difficulty; of education for the 'norm', of selection criteria, of the 11+, comparing individual with others; of a narrow definition of what 'education' was about. Moreover, with the emphasis on parental choice, this meant greater power to those parents who knew how to choose and felt empowered to make that choice. Some children have such a well coordinated parental lobby — the dyslexic, the physically disabled, those with partial sight, for instance — but some do not. 'Naughty' children are bad news in such a market economy. No one wants them. They are bad for the image of the school, they are bad for the league tables, they are difficult and time-consuming, they upset and stress the teachers. Their difference is intolerable.

As one headteacher speaking on the BBC *Panorama* programme in 1993 has so aptly suggested 'we have, through the ethos of the educational market economy, created human unsaleable goods'. They are stuck on our shelves, unwanted and going fast past their best. They look bad for the image. They need 'clearing out'.

The parents of many behaviourally difficult children may themselves be unable or unwilling to support their child. Often they are not familiar with procedures and bureaucracy. Almost always they themselves are disempowered to make a fuss, or to appeal — they often feel guilty — or made to feel to blame — for their children's behaviour. They often feel bewildered or belligerent at the way their children are being treated. Moreover, the professionals in the system often feel helpless over these children. They, too, have little clout in a school's decision to exclude. They know of the paucity of alternatives available. They, too, are pressed for time with a multitude of demands from a wide range of children and family needs. They, too, often find these children difficult and demanding and solutions slow to find. So, even from the 'natural' advocates within the system from which a special child might reasonably expect support, it might well not be forthcoming.

Behaviourally difficult children are, in short, already a vulnerable group within our schools — already hampered by a variety of emotional and behavioural difficulties. What I suggest the recent political developments have done is to render this already vulnerable group even more vulnerable — vulnerable to exclusion, vulnerable to underresourced alternatives, vulnerable to having their rights to 'education' in its fullest sense, abused.

So, we have a scenario — a sociopolitical climate which actually renders a group of our children vulnerable to abuse. Special needs children within a market economy are bad news. One cannot make a profit out of children with difficulties — especially behavioural difficulties.

Trends in Exclusions

In 1992 I carried out a survey of trends in exclusions in one area within a rural local authority in Britain. A range of schools were represented — city comprehensives, rural comprehensives, primary and special schools. The figures (available from the author) showed quite clearly the ever upward trend in the number of exclusions suggesting an increasing tendency for schools to seek exclusion as a solution to the problem of disruptive pupils.

There was a consistent decrease in the exclusion figures during the spring term followed by the sharp increase in the summer term. This apparent anomaly might be explained by the fact that schools' capitation day is during the spring term. Therefore, it suits schools, financially, to have as many pupils as possible at this point of census, as each child represents income for the school. However, after this time, the school can exclude any undesirables with alacrity — they do not then lose the money, only the 'pain in the neck'.

Other trends that should be noted. Some schools 'hold on' better to their pupils than others and are 'less exclusive'. Is this because they have less disruptive children than other schools, a different catchment area and intake, or is it because of a different set of attitudes, a different policy towards disruption? For instance, the figures showed that one particular rural comprehensive excludes proportionately more pupils than any of its inner-city counterparts and even more than a similarly placed school that happens to be one of the largest comprehensives in the country.

There was also an increase in the number of primary schools excluding children, even small, rural ones — hitherto an unknown phenomena. Historically such schools would often have held on and worked with even the most difficult children as part of a caring, inclusive community. Furthermore some special schools had began to exclude children — even those designed to cater for children with emotional and behavioural difficulties.

These figures strongly suggest that our entire education system — even those parts designed to cater for children with emotional and behavioural difficulties, are becoming increasingly intolerant and exclusive.

At the time of the study a total of eighty children were excluded from schools in this one area of the LEA. Of these twenty-one were placed in an exclusion unit which is reserved for year 11 children only. Forty were receiving three hours of home teaching per week and the remainder were divided between a psychiatric unit or a short stay facility provided by the social services.

In general the provision for our excluded children was less than satisfactory. It was underresourced, facilities were poor, the teachers were inexperienced or 'rusty', there was little LEA support, no psychiatric and little psychological input and schools were increasingly reluctant to have the children back. The exclusion unit was not even officially deemed 'special' education for the purposes of its budgetary allocation.

Even those children for whom the LEA were fulfilling their statutory obligations — those in the Unit and those on home tuition — one could query just how much of their academic, social, emotional and behavioural needs were being met in three hours a week. And what about their 'spiritual, moral and cultural' needs called for in the National Curriculum?

Is it not ironic that, at a time when society, Government, lawyers, parents and others are calling for greater moral awareness and there is a growing concern over the behaviour of our young people, we are actually increasing the likelihood of delinquent behaviour by:

(i)   increasingly excluding our adolescents from the very means by which some of this awareness and behaviour could be learnt;

(ii)   alienating them even more from society by underlining their non-acceptability and by modelling intolerance and exclusion as a solution to problems;

(iii) giving them so little to do with their time that vast amounts of their week are spent aimlessly.

These three factors together create an explosive and dangerous cocktail. Wragg (1992) reiterates this point — 'if we now have a destructive, alienated, apparently immoral youth roaming our streets, then maybe we have only ourselves to blame'.

Local management of schools opting-out and selection criteria all contribute to render certain children at risk. Giving schools greater responsibility allows more choice. Indeed this is, of course, the Government's intention. But choice is always a matter of a moral dilemma. There has to be criteria to guide the choice, and they themselves are value-laden and, as such, reflect a school's vision.

I believe the 1988 Act presented schools, parents and administrators with what were essentially moral choices. At the time they were seen as primarily financial choices — I would suggest that over the issue of disruptive children, we are now reaping the effects of having ignored, ducked or misconstrued the very essence of the task ahead of us. Nothing in the 1993 Act would indicate a reversal of this trend.

Discussion

What we have then, I would suggest, is a scandal of systemic abdication of responsibility. Certain children, it would seem, are not wanted. They do not fit

— behaviourally, socially or emotionally. Schools — successfully — get rid of them. Some headteachers talk of 'clearing them out'. Others refer to their 'right' to exclude — 'if I'm running a business', said one, 'yes, I must exclude those who reduce my profitability'. They are 'passengers dragging you back'.

I have outlined a political/legislative climate that certainly sheds some understanding on why schools are excluding, but, if we acknowledge that there is still an element of choice, they do not *have* to. They could seek other solutions. The chosen route is itself a product of attitudes and values. Why, then, might we be excluding more children than ever from our schools, and by implication, from our society?

A Systemic Interpretation

Exclusivity, intolerance, 'getting rid of', 'not my responsibility' blame are all symptoms of projection — projected guilt. Guilt over dilemmas we don't know how to solve, of feeling overwhelmed and powerless; of the fears, anxieties and anger that challenging and difficult behaviour presents us with. Guilt at knowing we should but we can't — don't have time, the resources, the supports, the skills, the will . . .

I believe that our excluded children — and indeed our EBD children in general — are at risk of becoming the scapegoats of a system that can't cope. A system that increasingly feels under pressure to meet a variety of conflicting demands in ever decreasing time deadlines. A system overwhelmed and failing in coping with its own change. At such a time, how much we need scapegoats. We choose as our scapegoats — as societies have immemorial — those who are clearly identifiable as different, the powerless, those with low self-esteem, failures, those with no advocates, those already with little . . . and then we cut them off from the very means of addressing those problems — both materially and procedurally — and thus contribute to their ever-spiralling problems of alienation, disaffection and delinquency.

We then blame each other (Government blames the church, parents blame teachers, social services blame education, etc.) and expect others to find a solution. A vain hope while each segment of the system is hooked into avoiding responsibility and thus projecting the guilt onto other groups.

We have, therefore, a series of systemic phenomena at each and every interface of the system. At a recent training day with a group of teachers from exclusion units, they reported feelings of 'frustration, anger, low self-esteem, disappointment, fear, puzzlement', and that things were 'unfair'. They felt 'unmotivated', 'wished to give up' and 'forgotten'. These were feelings they had about the children at the unit, but also about the way they were treated by the local authority. In identifying *their* responses, the teachers quickly said how much more they could understand the children and their feelings in the situation in which the children found themselves.

This idea of what I have termed **systemic reciprocity** (Parffrey, 1993)

— that feelings, pathologies or tasks identified at one interface of a system, can be useful predictors as to what is happening or needs to happen at another interface — is, I believe, a useful hypothesis generator in systems research. Its usefulness and application to the issue of exclusion continues to be explored.

The Way Forward?

Using this idea of reciprocity to find a way forward out of this systemic impasse, we need to tackle the problem at each and every interface of the system. We *all* contribute to the problem of excluded children. We need first to acknowledge that our children's behaviour is *our* responsibility — we have a corporate responsibility for their behaviour and how we deal with it. Within any particular sub-system of society, therefore, like education, we can identify the parts of that system that need to recognize and 'own' that responsibility.

The parent, the classroom teacher, the headteacher, the school psychologist, the officers of the LEA are but just some of the education system that traditionally point fingers at one another and 'blame' for the problems of failing children. But any sub-system itself is embedded with a broader context — of our sub-systems, for example, of social services and health and within the broader national climate of political, social and moral attitudes.

I believe that, if we are to begin to solve the problem of excluded children (and by implication, that of delinquent and disaffected children), then each part of this system must cooperate and pull together.

At a local level, staff, parents, management and administrators need to work together with a common commitment to stick with it and the child, until the problem is solved. A high level of communication and, yes, confrontation, will be necessary if the conflict of views is to be resolved. There needs to be a common will to find a solution and sufficient resources to provide it.

At an administrative level, the different statutory services need to work together in the interests of the child — health, social services, and education need to see themselves as complementary in meeting children's and families' needs, rather than as competitors.

Recent work supported by the Rowntree Foundation concluded that 'It is important that an inter agency approach to work with adolescents is adopted'. The research has shown that when agencies engage in boundary disputes, the delay that ensues can create a desperate situation for families, and it is only when a serious incident or offence happens that any agency is forced to take responsibility (Rowntree Project, 1993).

Schools need to:

- establish clear and communicable *discipline policies* and procedures of which exclusion is quite explicitly the last step;
- involve parents and the pupil at an early stage as *partners* with the school in generating solutions;
- involve support services at an early stage to design preventative

strategies and to be involved in decision-making about exclusion and future placement;

- continue to liaise with the agency offering support *after* exclusion by providing information, resources and examination facilities;
- where appropriate, a phased *return* to the school could be planned.

Agencies need to:

- set up multi-agency groups to coordinate policy, procedure and practice both of preventative strategies and of crisis intervention. Such bodies would need to function at each administrative level to provide coherence across schools and across areas.

Units need to:

- 'Retrack' as a way of rebuilding records on individuals with sometimes multiple-school histories, but also as a form of therapeutic intervention. Similar to 'life-story work', it may aid the young person to begin to tell a coherent life story and, in making sense of their past, begin to build an identity and self-esteem for the present, and so be able to envisage for themselves a future. Such work leads naturally to goal-setting and action planning. This is at present being tried, with some success, by the South Devon team of educational psychologists.

These are just some of the ideas emerging from this Rowntree research. Enquiries continue with groups of teachers, unit staff, LEA officers and support services, in the search for, and development of, good practice in dealing with and preventing exclusion.

At a national level, we need a greater understanding of the issues and a will to stick with the complexities and look for long-term prevention, rather than knee-jerk reactions more to do with vengeance and control. Public perceptions are, as we have seen, crucial in both contributing to the problem but also, therefore, in finding a solution.

Exclusion, it seems, is a matter of *attitudes*. Our attitudes to children who misbehave, our attitudes to the staff and schools who try and cater for their needs, our attitudes to the parents of such children, our attitudes to how we think they should be treated. Some countries see exclusion as a denial of human rights and do not allow schools to exclude any children. Canada, for instance, and the USA, do not exclude children — they expect and support their schools to find alternative, in-house solutions to the problems of disruptive behaviour.

In this country it is still optional. The pre-1988 spirit was very much to try and find in-school solutions to disruption. Nowadays, it may seem overly time-consuming to do so, or at worst, according to the BBC *Panorama* programme, headteachers who do not exclude are seen as weak and ineffectual by their staff.

Alternatively, we can look to charity. Are 'educational soup-kitchens' the answer for our excluded children? If we have, indeed, through the market economy, created human unsaleable goods, then perhaps the Salvation Army — or church schools — or industry — should salvage what society has rendered unwanted? Or is charity itself yet a further symptom of a failed society?

The question is, just whose responsibility are these children?

At a conference on issues of politics and vulnerable children Holman (1993) suggested that long-term solutions are needed for society's values to change — he suggested that, in our poor and our excluded, we were 'prostituting moral principles for economic profit'. I, too, have previously suggested that school psychologists, as but one agent of our educational system, do sometimes 'prostitute themselves to the pimp of the LEA' (Parffrey, 1989, private correspondence). We often try and remain amoral and non-engaged when faced with bureaucratic decisions with which we disagree. But what price integrity? It is sometimes difficult to remain true to one's professional principles when one's job is at stake, but we will need, I suggest, each to reassess our values and attitudes towards certain of our young people if we are to solve the problem of exclusion.

Holman (1993) argues that if our values are to change and therefore solutions to be found:

(i)   we need a corporate will and a clarity of purpose and priorities;
(ii) we need to wed the personal and the public;
(iii) we need the material and social resources to be made available;
(iv) above all, we need a spirit of fraternity — of sharing, participative partnership *with* those with difficulties, of community development and support, of the different parts of the system working cooperatively.

I hope I have argued that it is exactly these factors that we need at every level and interface of our society, if the problem of excluded children is to be ameliorated and if they are to have rightful access to their needs as adolescents — to belong, to be valued and to contribute.

References

ELTON REPORT (1989) *Discipline in Schools*, London, HMSO.
HOLMAN, R. (1993) 'A vulnerable class of children', *Educational and Child Psychology*, **10**, 3, pp. 47–56.
PARFFREY, V. (1990) 'Tor Hill: An alternative to exclusion?', *Journal of the Association of Educational Psychologists*, **5**, 4, pp. 216–22.
PARFFREY, V. (1993) *'Changing schools: Myth or reality'*, unpublished PhD thesis, University of Exeter.
ROWNTREE PROJECT (1993) *Young People in Difficulties*, Oxford, Rowntree Trust.
WRAGG, E. (1992) 'Seeds of destruction being sown in a three-class system', *The Observer*, 17 May.

Chapter 11

Pastoral Care and Black Pupils: an Uneasy Relationship

Kenneth McIntyre

Pastoral care as practised in British schools purports to be the system through which strategies that facilitate the learning, welfare and well-being of pupils are implemented. Its purpose is said to facilitate pupils' access to educational opportunities available in the curriculum offered (Clemett and Pearce, 1986). As such it encompasses several traditional dimensions of school life including the ethos of the school, personal and social education, vocational guidance, counselling and welfare of pupils and administration. The pastoral curriculum and the academic curriculum form the major provision in schools for the education of all pupils.

The notion that schools should offer a curriculum which is more broadly based than a limited consideration of subject teaching, is enshrined in the definition of the National Curriculum:

> The curriculum for a maintained school satisfies the requirements of this section if it is a balanced and broadly based curriculum which
>
> > (a) promotes the spiritual, moral, cultural, mental and physical well-being of pupils at the school and of society; and
> > (b) prepares such pupils for the opportunities, responsibilities and experience of adult life. (DES, 1988, section 1, para. 2)

Those aims can be viewed as incorporating a more pastorally orientated perspective than previous education acts and is clearer in the view that the tasks of schools should involve a wider view of pupils' preparation for adult life and responsibilities (Marland, 1989).

To understand the issues leading up to this declaration of the importance of this task and the effectiveness of its implementation with black pupils (pupils of African/Caribbean heritage) in the school life, it is first necessary to explore the development of pastoral care as a system of support.

History of Pastoral Care

The idea that schools and teachers should have both 'caring' and 'teaching' responsibilities, precedes the introduction of compulsory schooling in the late nineteenth century. Caring within schools has a complex history. It probably became identified with the role of these early teachers as they became involved with the social, personal and more than likely the religious and moral development of their pupils as part of teaching a variety of subjects to pupils from a broader social catchment. Teaching was viewed not just as the passing on of certain skills and knowledge, but also as the inculcation of acceptable attitudes, behaviours and the 'moulding' of young minds to suit the demands of a society in rapid change towards industrialization (Clemett and Pearce, 1986).

At the time the 1944 Education Act was introduced, it was already a well established practice that headteachers had the important task of looking after the 'welfare' of pupils in schools. The interaction and practice changed considerably over the following decades so that by the 1950s with the introduction of comprehensive education and large purpose built schools needed to deliver a more subject-based curriculum, there was already a need to devise active systems of support and guidance for pupils.

As the move towards comprehensive education increased with the creation of these new schools, trends began to emerge which significantly affected the organization of care and guidance within schools. There was a need for more formal systems of support for pupils which would also complement subject-teaching as this was now increasingly organized on a 'year-group' basis. The organization of pastoral care therefore changed from the more traditional 'house system' to a 'year system'. The former offered a mixed-aged or vertical model of delivery and allowed whole families of pupils to be kept together pastorally regardless of age. The latter was based on a horizontal system which was modelled on year groupings and in this way mirrored the organization and delivery of the academic curriculum. A number of authors cynically regarded the development of this system of pastoral care as merely based on expedience and saw two factors 'diversity and size' as the main influence (Marland, 1974; Lang, 1984).

In the early 1980s that aspect of life had begun to move from its original focus on individuals and had begun to emphasize the need for group activity and interaction. From the literature, it is likely that the large size of schools made this focus on group work necessary if teachers were to influence significantly the personal and social development of their pupils (Bulman and Jenkins, 1988). This concept of personal and social education as a distinct feature of pastoral care gave rise to the development of a 'pastoral curriculum' which could be taught (Marland, 1980; Best and Ribbins, 1983).

The need for a pastoral 'curriculum' resulted in many publications which attempted to promote that aspect of the school's curriculum as another subject (Marland, 1980). Amongst them, were schemes by Baldwin and Wells (1979);

Hamblin (1978) and Foster (1988). These publications, in particular those by Baldwin and by Foster, contained units of work which the authors intended to be applied 'developmentally' and used as textbooks with pupils throughout their secondary school life.

More recently, the trend has been for schools to produce their own 'in-house' schemes which would give schools opportunities to reflect the demands and needs of their own pupil population their environment and perceptions of their staff. It was thought likely that those schemes, more than the celebrated mass-produced publications, would take into account the multicultural/multiracial backgrounds of pupils which became established dimensions of school-life by the 1970s and 1980s but there has been no wide scale evaluation to assess whether or not this has happened (Duncan, 1988).

However, since its rapid expansion in the late 1960s, the general practice of pastoral care, has been a relatively neglected aspect of research into school life (Marland, 1985). From the available studies, a number of observations can be used to support the view and lend weight to the suspicion that its development has not been informed by widescale evaluation nor influenced by the needs of pupils and outcomes of its intervention on their behalf. These would include:

(i)   the lack of widespread evaluative research in the field (Marland, 1974; Clemett and Pearce, 1986; McIntyre, 1990);

(ii) its subservient role when compared with the academic curriculum (McIntyre, 1990);

(iii) its function as a mechanism of control (Williamson, 1980; Raymond, 1985);

(iv) the lack of training of staff (Best and Maher, 1984; Raymond, 1985);

(v)   the poor status of pastoral care staff compared with that of subject teachers in secondary schools (Raymond, 1985; Clemett and Pearce, 1986).

These issues were of general concern to researchers in the field of pastoral care because of their impact on the lives of all pupils. However there was even more specific concern with regards to the pastoral needs of black pupils in secondary schools since this group was already being highlighted elsewhere as experiencing many difficulties at school. The relative absence of pastoral literature exploring these issues was reported:

> The relationship between pastoral care and the educational needs of ethnic minority children and of the whole population of pupils with regards to their perspective of a multiethnic society, is a major and urgent focus for educational research. (Marland, 1985, p. 89)

Marland's observations underlined the serious neglect of these issues, both in terms of the literature on pastoral care, and of general evaluations based on content, aims and outcomes of such programmes. His criticisms of the lack of consideration within widescale studies, surveys and evaluations of the educational experiences of black pupils in British schools went further. He did not consider the Swann Report (Swann, 1985) nor other studies of black pupils to be 'illuminating', and argued that Swann in particular showed a poor understanding of the broad features of pastoral care by solely restricting its discussion to that of school rules regarding uniform and the need for separate showers. There was a lack of a wider and more critical analysis of the conceptualization and organization of this very important aspect of school provision (see Marland, 1985, p. 88; and Swann, 1985, pp. 203 and 513).

In response to this omission other writers in the field sought to articulate the need for additional dimensions to pastoral care to address this group. A review of some of the articles published in this field of study confirmed this view of neglect and oversight (Goodhew, 1987). Furthermore, multicultural education and pastoral care seemed to develop independently of one another. Authors became bolder in their statement that 'pastoral care was part of the structure which disenfranchises black pupils' (Garnet and Lang, 1986). Another study found that black pupils in a sample of schools from the Midlands did not perceive pastoral care 'as relevant to them' (Woods, 1984).

More recent articles began to add the knowledge and perceptions in this very important field by considering the relationship and implications of developments in the field of multicultural education as they affect pastoral care development and provision. They concluded that such provision and development would gain considerably from being associated more strongly and by being better coordinated with each other (Garnet and Lang, 1986; Pelleschi, 1986; Scadding, 1988; Singh, 1988; McIntyre, 1990).

These early stirrings helped to focus on the experiences of black pupils and to highlight the shortcomings of the support offered to them.

The Experiences of Black Children

Recent evaluations of pastoral care in relation to the experiences of black pupils concluded that, overall, the experiences of this group of pupils were qualitatively and significantly different than that of their white peers (McIntyre, 1990). The empirical evidence of these differences can be summarized to show that:

(i) black pupils are perceived as less motivated in school (Verma, 1986);

(ii) the successes of black pupils are thought more likely to be in the 'social' aspects of life for example, sport and music and not in the non-academic aspects of the curriculum (Figueroa, 1984);

(iii) teachers stereotype black pupils more negatively than white pupils (Willey, 1984; Figueroa, 1984; Swann, 1985; Verma, 1988);

(iv)   black pupils have a different opinion of and relationship with teachers, for example, they perceive teachers as less supportive (Rampton, 1981; Tomlinson, 1984; Swann, 1985; Verma, 1988);

(v)   racism is an important but neglected issue in the difficulties that black pupils encounter in school (Willey, 1984; Figueroa, 1984; Verma, 1986; Newsan, 1988);

(vi)   black pupils have greater difficulties in developing a healthy self-concept/esteem (Stone, 1981; Figueroa, 1984, p. 119; Verma, 1986);

(vii)   black pupils are more likely to be excluded/transferred as a method of resolving difficulties in school (Rampton, 1981; Tomlinson, 1983a);

(viii)   research indicates that schools respond less positively/quickly with problems experienced by black pupils (Rampton, 1981; Willey, 1984; Swann, 1985; Wright, 1987; Kelly and Cohn, 1988);

(ix)   schools are less likely to involve black parents in partnerships to solving problems their children encounter at school (Tomlinson, 1984; Kelly and Cohn, 1988; Tomlinson and Smith, 1989);

(x)   schools are less likely to incorporate outside agencies, for example psychological services, except as a means of 'removing' black pupils. The research indicates that black pupils are placed in 'special provision' much more quickly than white pupils (Rampton, 1981; Tomlinson, 1983b);

(xi)   black parents appear to have a more positive attitude to their children's education than white parents (Tomlinson, 1983a, 1983b and 1984; Swann, 1985; Tomlinson and Smith, 1989);

(xii)   schools are generally less supportive of the educational success of black pupils than white pupils (Verma, 1986; Tomlinson, 1984; Swann, 1985; Wright, 1987);

(xiii)   schools are less likely to 'believe' and facilitate the views of black pupils in times of conflict (Rampton, 1981; Swann, 1985; Verma, 1988);

(xiv)   school staff are less likely to appreciate and be skilled in ways of motivating black pupils (Rampton, 1981; Tomlinson, 1984; Verma, 1986);

(xv)   special schools are more often sought as options for dealing with the difficulties of black pupils rather than counselling or other forms of support (Rampton, 1981; Tomlinson, 1983; Figueroa, 1984; Jeffcoate, 1984);

(xvi)   schools are less able to support the academic abilities of black pupils through not understanding how black pupils learn (Figueroa, 1984; Tomlinson, 1984; Swann, 1985; Verma, 1986; Mackintosh, 1988);

(xvii)   schools are not well placed to develop the academic success of black pupils because of poor expectation from teachers (Rampton, 1981; Tomlinson, 1984; Verma, 1986; Mackintosh, 1988);

(xviii) there is much evidence to show that black pupils in general underachieve academically (Figueroa, 1984; Verma, 1986; Swann, 1985);

(xix) negative stereotyping affects the performance and the quality of support given (Willey, 1984; Figueroa, 1984; Swann, 1985; Verma, 1988);

(xx) black pupils do not receive vocational guidance which assists the realization of their ambitions (Rampton, 1981; Ali *et al.*, 1987; Department of Employment, 1990);

(xxi) the pastoral curriculum very often does not reflect the presence of black pupils in schools and society. It does not reflect the achievements of black people as a historical fact (Bulman and Jenkins, 1988; Duncan, 1988);

(xxii) many educationalists and teachers consider black pupils underachieve because they are not intelligent (Mackintosh and Mascie-Taylor, 1981; in Swann, 1985).

These issues summarized from research over the last fifteen years offer negative outcomes and emphasize the ineffectiveness of pastoral care systems in particular, to improve the educational well-being of black pupils. New strategies need to be developed if improvements are to be made.

Some Ways Forward

These are focused mainly on what schools should usefully consider in order to offer a more positive direction to the implementation of a pastoral care policy which would begin to address the needs of black pupils. The list is not exhaustive.

(i) Personal and social education as part of pastoral care provision must be considered as 'the most important of the cross-curricular dimensions' (Elton, 1989) and that it should be the responsibility of all teachers. This would have implications for the training of teachers in all aspects of motivating, guiding and counselling black pupils.

(ii) All schools with substantial numbers of black pupils should have access to specialist support and input from black professional staff to assist the development and evaluation of these strategies and to offer black pupils specialized help.

(iii) These schools should reflect the presence of black pupils in its development of a positive learning ethos. For example, the achievements of famous black people should be reflected in school adornments. Racist language and abuse from both staff and pupils should be rejected. Teachers should take seriously the complaints of black pupils about racial abuse.

(iv)   There should be a clear discipline code for the whole school. 'Assertive discipline' is a strategy which provides one way forward (Canter, 1984).

(v)   Black pupils and their parents should be involved in the development of these strategies (McIntyre, 1990).

(vi)   There should be a system of mentoring within schools which would provide suitable role models for black pupils.

(vii) Teachers should be offered the time to pursue these duties and should receive additional training specific to working with black pupils.

(viii) The availability of current literature and research on the psychological development of black children should be improved in schools.

(ix)   There should be projects started within schools which address the specific social and identity needs of black pupils. The Oxford Project is a good example of such a strategy (Sallion-James, 1993).

Conclusion

Black pupils are failing within British schools and the implementation of the Education Reform Act has not indicated that this situation will improve without considerable effort and expertise (Department for Education, 1993). Moreover, pastoral care as a system of support within schools is specifically failing in its function to promote the learning and social development of this group of pupils. Traditional pastoral care has therefore to be considered as a flawed response and largely irrelevant as a means of intervention when black pupils encounter difficulties in their schooling. The use of this system as a 'police force' in the process of removing disaffected pupils has to be reexamined and radically changed if it is to attract any credibility. New directions and strategies have to be devised as a matter of urgency if pastoral care is to be an effective system of intervention and support for black pupils.

References

ALI, N., COOK, J. and RYAN, A. (1987) 'Processing black clients: A careers service perspective', in CROSS, M. and SMITH, D. (Eds) *Black Youth Futures — Ethnic Minorities and the YT Schemes*, Leicester, NYB.

BALDWIN, J. and WELLS, H. (1979) *Active Tutorial Work, Books 1 to 5*, Oxford, Blackwell.

BEST, R. (1988) 'Care and control — Are we getting it right?', *Pastoral Care in Education*, **6**, 2, pp. 2–9.

BEST, R. and MAHER, P. (1984) *Training and Support for Pastoral Care*, London, NAPC.

BEST, R. and RIBBINS, P. (1983) 'Rethinking the pastoral-academic split', *Pastoral Care in Education*, **1**, 1, pp. 12–16.

BULMAN, L. and JENKINS, D. (1988) *The Pastoral Curriculum*, London, Blackwell.

CANTER, L. (1984) *Assertive Discipline*, Santa Monica, CA, Lee Canter and Associates.

CLEMETT, A.J. and PEARCE, J.S. (1986) *The Evaluation of Pastoral Care*, London, Blackwell.

DEPARTMENT FOR EDUCATION (1993) *Access and Achievement In Urban Education*, London, HMSO.

DEPARTMENT OF EDUCATION AND SCIENCE (1988) *The Education Reform Act*, London, HMSO.

DEPARTMENT OF EMPLOYMENT (1990) 'Ethnic minorities and the careers service: An investigation into the process of assessment and placement', *Department of Employment Research Paper Series No. 73*, London, HMSO.

DUNCAN, C. (1988) *Pastoral Care: An Anti-Racist/Multicultural Perspective*, Oxford, Blackwell.

ELTON, LORD (1989) *Discipline in Schools: Report of the Committee of the Enquiry*, London, HMSO.

FIGUEROA, P. (1984) 'Minority pupils' progress', in CRAFT, M. (Ed) *Education and Cultural Pluralism*, Lewes, Falmer Press.

FOSTER, J. (1988) *Lifelines*, London, Collins Educational.

GARNET, B. and LANG, P. (1986) 'Pastoral care and multiracial education', *Pastoral Care In Education*, **4**, 3, pp. 158–64.

GOODHEW, E. (1987) 'Personal and social education and race', *Pastoral Care In Education*, **5**, 3, pp. 16–24.

HAMBLIN, D.H. (1978) *The Teacher and Pastoral Care*, London, Blackwell.

JEFFCOATE, R. (1984) *The Ethnic Minorities and Education*, London, Harper Educationa' Series.

KELLY, E. and COHN, T. (1988) *Racism in Schools — New Research Evidence*, London, Trentham Books.

LANG, P. (1984) 'Pastoral care: Some reflections on possible influences', *Pastoral Care in Education*, **2**, 2, pp. 136–46.

MCINTYRE, K. (1990) 'The pastoral needs of black pupils', unpublished PhD thesis, University of Manchester.

MACKINTOSH, N.J. and MASCIE-TAYLOR, C.G.N. (1981) 'The IQ question', in SWANN, M. (1985) *The Swann Report — Education For All: Report Of the Committee Of Inquiry Into The Education Of Children From Ethnic Minority Groups*, London, HMSO.

MACKINTOSH, N.J. (1988) 'West Indian and Asian children's educational attainment', in VERMA, G. and PUMFREY, P. (Eds) *Educational Attainments: Issues and Outcomes*, London, Falmer Press.

MARLAND, M. (1974) *Pastoral Care*, London, Heinemann.

MARLAND, M. (1980) 'The pastoral curriculum', in BEST, R. (Ed) *Perspectives on Pastoral Care*, London, Heinemann.

MARLAND, M. (1985) 'Parents, schooling and the welfare of pupils', in RIBBINS, P. (Ed) *Schooling And Welfare*, Lewes, Falmer Press.

MARLAND, M. (1989) 'Shaping and delivering pastoral care: The new opportunities', *Journal of Pastoral Care*, pp. 14–21.

NEWSAN, P. (1988) 'Policies and promising practices in education', in VERMA, G. and PUMFREY, P. (Eds) *Educational Attainments: Issues and Outcomes*, London, Falmer Press.

PELLESCHI, A. (1986) 'Screening pupils in a multicultural school', *Pastoral Care In Education*, **4**, 3, pp. 148–58.

RAMPTON, A. (1981) *The Rampton Report. West Indian Children in Our Schools. Interim Report of Enquiry into Education of Children from Ethnic Minority Groups*, London, HMSO.

RAYMOND, J. (1985) *Implementing Pastoral Care in Schools*, London, Croom Helm.

SCADDING, H. (1988) 'Anti-racism in schools: A discussion of the difficulties a pastoral care team may face in promoting anti-racist policies and practices', *Pastoral Care in Education*, **6**, 1, pp. 16–22.

SALLION-JAMES, D. (1993) 'Higher attainment/pastoral project', *Multicultural Education*, **12**, 1, pp. 16–22.

SINGH, B. (1988) 'The black perspective of anti-racism in schools', *Pastoral Care In Education*, **6**, 4, pp. 14–16..

STONE, M. (1981) *The Education of Black Child in Britain: The Myth of Multiracial Education*, Glasgow, Fontana.

SWANN, M. (1985) *The Swann Report. Education For All: Report Of The Committee of Inquiry Into the Education of Children From Ethnic Minority Groups*, London, HMSO.

TOMLINSON, S. (1983a) 'The educational performance of minority children', *New Community*, **8**, 3, pp. 136–45.

TOMLINSON, S. (1983b) *Ethnic Minorities in British Schools — A Review of the Literature 1960–1982*, London, Policy Studies Institute/Heinemann Educational.

TOMLINSON, S. (1984) *Home and School in Multicultural Britain*, London, Batstold.

TOMLINSON, S. and SMITH, D.J. (1989) *The School Effect: A Study of Multicultural Comprehensives*, London, Policy Studies Institute.

VERMA, G.K. (1986) (Ed) *Ethnicity and Educational Achievement in British Schools*, London, Macmillan.

VERMA, G.K. and PUMFREY, P. (Eds) (1988) *Educational Attainments: Issues and Outcomes*, London, Falmer Press.

WILLEY, R. (1984) *Race, Equality and Schools*, London, Methuen.

WILLIAMSON, D. (1980) 'Pastoral care or pastoralization?', in BEST, R. (Ed) *Perspectives on Pastoral Care*, London, Heinemann.

WOODS, E. (1984) 'The practice of pastoral care in an urban comprehensive school', *Pastoral Care In Education*, **12**, 3, pp. 17–21.

WRIGHT, C. (1987) 'Black students — White teachers', in TROYNA, B. (Ed) *Racial Inequality In Education*, London, Tavistock Publications.

Chapter 12

Developing an LEA Strategy for Meeting Emotional and Behavioural Difficulties: Policy and Practice

---

Gareth Price and John Cousil

This chapter describes the work which has been ongoing in Tameside, a small metropolitan borough in Greater Manchester, over the past five years or so in developing a special educational needs (SEN) policy and service delivery model to help implement that policy. It also outlines how the policy and model are being applied in attempting to ensure that pupils with emotional and/or behavioural difficulties are gaining access to a relevant and high quality education.

Establishing a Policy to Guide Subsequent Service Delivery

Back in 1987 when a group of Council members and LEA officers first met to share views on the issue of an LEA SEN Policy, it was generally agreed that a clear policy statement was essential to guide any future development of special provision. Further discussion subsequently helped arrive at the view that the people of Tameside should be consulted on and have an opportunity to comment on three key issues, namely:

(i) the definition of SEN which should guide policy development and related procedures;

(ii) the basic principles or 'shared values' which should act as the foundation for reviewing existing services and developing new services for meeting SEN;

(iii) the policy objectives which should give direction to and guide future service delivery models.

As a result of the ensuing consultation exercise, the LEA now has a definition of SEN which encompasses exceptional differences and not just exceptional difficulties. It aims to respect the fact that special needs may arise from a wide range of causal factors and not just learning difficulties or impairments.

It was also made clear within the basic principles which form the foundation for the policy that, wherever practicable, children and young people should be educated with others of their own age in their local community, ideally within their local mainstream school. However, the policy also recognizes that there will be circumstances where special provision for certain more complex special needs has to be made in special resourced schools. It further recognizes that in exceptional cases, some pupils may need to be educated in special schools outside the LEA because of the nature of their special needs.

As regards the types of establishments which should make special provision, it was felt that there was a continuing role for special schools, but that a more structured link was needed with mainstream schools if the wide range of pupils' special needs were to be addressed sensitively and flexibly.

Entitlement and Accountability

Much of the thinking linked to developing the LEA strategy for SEN has also been guided by two groups of principles associated with pupil entitlement and education service accountability. The principles of entitlement are embedded in a firm conviction that all pupils, whatever their individual needs, are entitled to a broad, balanced and relevant education which is differentiated to meet their individual needs, and enables them to:

  (i)   gain access to relevant educational experiences and learning opportunities;
 (ii)   acquire relevant information and knowledge;
(iii)   develop a relevant understanding of educational concepts;
 (iv)   develop relevant abilities, skills and competencies; and
  (v)   be able to reflect on their educational experiences in order to develop attitudes and values which are consistent with being members of a modern society.

The principles of accountability are embedded in a firm conviction that education services are accountable for delivering services in the most effective and efficient way to enable all pupils to access their educational entitlement. Accountability entails having positive strategies for:

  (i)   identifying the individual needs of all pupils;
 (ii)   assessing individuals to guide their future educational provision;
(iii)   planning and making provision consistent with meeting individual needs;
 (iv)   monitoring and recording individual progress;
  (v)   evaluating and reviewing individual progress;
 (vi)   providing meaningful information for clients and other appropriate individuals or organizations on the pupil's progress; and then
(vii)   using the results of reviews to guide future educational provision.

Further work on the principles of entitlement and accountability led to the LEA making explicit ten basic principles which should help guide the delivery of an entitlement curriculum. These are:

1 Clear teaching and learning objectives

   The need to have clear teaching objectives, described as 'Intended Learning Outcomes', and set in discrete units of study which are explicit to all concerned.

2 Realistic targets

   The need to set realistic targets in providing learning opportunities which are focused on individual needs and can be seen as both meaningful and relevant by each pupil.

3 Pupil involvement in own target-setting

   The need to involve pupils in their own target-setting wherever possible; aimed at goals which are attainable with reasonable effort on the part of each pupil.

4 Individual and group problem-solving

   The need to encourage both individual and group problem-solving strategies using a variety of teaching and learning styles.

5 Ongoing assessment

   The need to incorporate ongoing assessment, with the assessment techniques, and monitoring and record-keeping procedures closely related to the curriculum content and integrated within the work programmes.

6 Open record-keeping

   The need to incorporate open record-keeping with staff, pupils and their parents/carers having ready access to records, and being encouraged to discuss freely with one another.

7 Frequent feedback

   The need to provide frequent feedback for pupils on their progress with opportunities for individual tutoring and counselling. Discussion on both progress and lack of progress should be conducted in a positive and constructive manner.

8   Rewarding effort

The need to reward effort as well as academic attainment. It is important to remember that pupils learn best when they are happy and feel secure in their educational risk-taking.

9   Noteworthy accreditation

The need to provide noteworthy accreditation in which all pupils can develop a sense of pride, self-esteem, and gain the respect of others.

10   Record of achievement

The need to provide a record of achievement which celebrates the overall achievements of all pupils in their educational endeavours.

Putting Policy into Practice

The next task, having established the policy to guide future developments, was to develop a service delivery model which would be sufficiently flexible to accommodate most areas of special needs. It also needed to allow a systematic and constructive link to be established between mainstream and special schools in providing a continuum of special provision. The continuum needed to be able to accommodate the wide range and levels of complexity of special needs.

A further consultation exercise in the LEA resulted in the Tameside Six Stage Continuum Model of SEN Service Delivery. Within each stage are defined the broad characteristics of the SEN which should be accommodated within that stage. These are outlined briefly below.

Stage One

The SEN are not exceptional in that they do not require any special provision beyond good mainstream differentiated classroom teaching and learning styles.

Stage Two

The SEN are exceptional in that they require the mainstream school to make special provision from within its own resources for an extended period of time. The school will open a 'School Internal Action File (SIAF)' within this stage, and set up 'Individual Action Plans (IAP)' at 'Action Planning Meetings (APM)' to plan the implementation, monitoring and evaluation of the special provision. The school's designated SEN Coordinator will oversee the IAPs, and monitor the pupil's progress in line with his/her SIAF.

Stage Three

The SEN are such that the mainstream school is concerned that it may not be able to meet the pupil's exceptional needs from within its own resources. At this stage the LEA becomes formally involved in monitoring the pupil's IAPs via the school's educational psychologist. (The psychologist may have been involved informally in previous discussions about the pupil, but it is at this stage that involvement becomes formalized). If concern continues within this stage, the LEA may be requested to initiate a statutory assessment of the pupil's special needs under the terms of the 1993 Education Act.

Stage Four (Tier One Statemented SEN Provision)

The SEN are such that they warrant a Statement of SEN. They are such that the pupil can continue to attend any mainstream school in the LEA with Outreach Special Support on a part-time basis from one or more SEN Specialist Support Services.

Stage Five

The SEN are such that they warrant a Statement of SEN. They are such that they require the pupil to attend a Specially Resourced Mainstream School where more frequent special support can be made available than at Stage 4 because a Special Resource Centre or Unit is located within the resourced school.

Stage Six

The SEN are such that they warrant a Statement of SEN. They are such that they require the pupil to attend a special school. Such pupils should also be provided with appropriate opportunities for part-time mainstream school experience. (Extra-district special schools are only used when appropriate provision cannot be made available within the LEA).

(*Note*: This six stage procedure was in operation at the time the DFE *Code of Practice on the Identification and Assessment of Special Educational Needs* was published (DFE, 1994). There is considerable overlap between the six stage model described above and the five stages of assessment outlined in the Code and therefore Tameside will have little difficulty in integrating the guidance in the Code into its own procedures.)

Applying the LEA Strategy to Meeting Emotional and Behavioural Difficulties

In line with its stated policy and service delivery model, Tameside reorganized its specialist provision for pupils with emotional and/or behavioural difficulties into one comprehensive service under one management structure.

The service in the main covers primary and secondary statemented provision together with non-statemented provision for pupils with school attendance problems or those who had been excluded from school. It also contributes to the statutory assessment procedures.

The service encompasses:

Dale Grove School — a 11–16 years EBD mixed secondary day school with forty-two places.

Bankside Tutorial Unit — a 4–11 years EBD mixed day unit with eighteen places.

Tameside Primary Outreach Support Service — a service which provides part-time outreach support for pupils with EBD in mainstream primary schools throughout Tameside.

Tameside Secondary Outreach Support Service — the LEA is in the process of developing a part-time outreach support service for pupils with EBD in mainstream high schools throughout Tameside.

Hyde Secondary Tutorial Unit — a year 11 unit for non attending or excluded pupils with eighteen places.

Tameside Attendance Support Centre — a short-term special centre to support pupils with attendance problems in years 6, 7, 8 and 9. The Centre has fourteen places.

The staffing of the service currently comprises twenty full-time equivalent staff, including a head and two deputies and five special support assistants (NNEBs).

A management team structure was established which consists of a head of service; deputy headteachers; and teachers-in-charge of each school/unit. The Management Team meets weekly, with each school/unit holding weekly staff meetings, and there being termly meetings for the whole Service.

Starting the New Service

It was decided in starting the new service to initially devote two professional development days to bring all the staff together in order to explore short-term requirements and any immediate operational issues. Matters revolved around timetabling, curriculum balance, financial resourcing and professional development needs. This initial coming together of all staff was also important in getting across the message that everyone within the service, whatever their role and responsibilities, was contributing to a much larger team which in one way or another complemented one another.

Each school/unit was given its own share of the service capitation budget, and a system of inter-unit curriculum support and resource sharing was established. A system of leasing was agreed for sharing computer hardware and software, and for accessing the specialist teaching facilities at Dale Grove School. Each activity aimed to convey the clear message that the service is a team and the resources of the service, wherever they are located, belong to the team.

Service Mission Statement

In bringing together quite a diverse range of services, it was important to establish a common purpose for the service to guide its future operational strategies. It was soon decided that the Service needed a 'Mission Statement' with which each component could identify. However, it was realized in addressing this task that each school/unit first needed to clarify its aims and objectives in meeting the special educational needs of the pupils and how these might then contribute to the overall effectiveness of the service.

Having undertaken this task, it was then possible to work towards putting together a Mission Statement which encompassed all the individual aims. The resulting Mission Statement is as follows:

- The Tameside EBD Specialist Support Services offer a special educational needs resource directed towards those pupils who present and experience social, emotional and behavioural difficulties. The Service provides a positive and varied learning environment across the age and ability range which will enable each pupil to maximize his or her potential for social, emotional, physical, spiritual and intellectual growth.

Curriculum Provision

The service curriculum provision was first interpreted from the perspective that Tameside LEA believes that every pupil is entitled to a broad, balanced and relevant education which is differentiated to meet his/her individual educational needs. Within the service, there is a variety of provision which varies in terms of type, breadth and balance depending upon the contribution expected of the service in meeting the needs of the individual pupil, the time available and the point at which pupils are considered to need the support of the service.

Listed below is the type of curriculum provision each component within the Service endeavours to provide:

Dale Grove School

Dale Grove School offers a broad, balanced and relevant curriculum for all pupils following the requirements of the 1988 Education Reform Act and the guidelines of the National Curriculum. The school is staffed to facilitate an individualized approach to the process of teaching and learning. Since 1989, the school has been able to meet all the requirements of the National Curriculum. Cross-curricular themes such as PSE, careers education, traffic education and information technology are built into the timetable, and all year 11 pupils are given a placement on the work experience scheme. All programmes of work are modular and fully differentiated to meet the wide range of abilities and aptitudes of the pupils. They are supplemented by a comprehensive intervention strategy aimed at helping those pupils who lack basic functional skills in literacy and numeracy to develop competency in these vital areas of communication. The opportunity is provided for all year 11 pupils to enter for GCSE examinations.

Bankside Tutorial Unit

Bankside Tutorial Unit offers primary-aged pupils who exhibit difficult behaviours the opportunity to settle into a calm and supportive educational environment. Pupils have individualized work programmes which cater for their particular needs. Bankside offers a broad, balanced and relevant curriculum which incorporates the National Curriculum subjects. Schemes of work are age appropriate and differentiated to accommodate the needs of each pupil.

Hyde Secondary Tutorial Unit

Pupils referred for placement at the Hyde Secondary Tutorial Unit are from a broad band of disaffected adolescents approaching or into their final twelve months of schooling. Their mainstream placement has been terminated and there is no suitable alternative mainstream placement available. The function of the Unit is to continue the pupil's education until their official leaving date and in the process provide a broad and relevant curriculum to meet the individual needs of the students and prepare them for the world of work. It is seen as essential that the learning environment is positive and supportive, and in the process of enabling the pupils to respect themselves, thereby encourage them to respect others. Personal and social education has a major role within the timetable. Emphasis is placed on developing self-awareness and self-esteem, both in recognizing and in owning problem areas. Pupils are offered the opportunity to acquire knowledge, skills and understanding necessary to enable them to make the best of themselves and to be of benefit to the whole community. This is done by setting consistent expectations, counselling, peer group evaluation, and individual assessment. Two staff members have had counselling training and are experienced in offering individual counselling to pupils.

Tameside Attendance Support Centre

The function of the Attendance Support Centre is to support pupils who are experiencing difficulty in maintaining full attendance in mainstream schools. The Centre was established seven years ago and works with pupils in years 6, 7, 8 and 9. The curriculum is designed specifically to allow the pupil to return to school and therefore access the National Curriculum. It is based on personal and social education, and to this end the teaching is carried out in small groups to enable pupils to contribute fully to this work. The curriculum, produced in collaboration with an LEA adviser, enables pupils to understand themselves more fully and consequently allows them to examine realistically their reasons for school non-attendance. The curriculum aims to develop self-confidence and problem solving strategies to ensure that regular school attendance becomes a manageable proposition. It is delivered as distinct programmes of work for two particular groups, 'Phase Change' and 'High School' pupils.

(1) *'Phase Change' Pupils* — This programme of work is offered to year 6 pupils. Some of these pupils have experienced problems of regular attendance at primary school, whilst others have raised professional concern regarding their ability to transfer successfully to high school. The curriculum prepares the pupils for their move to high school and visits to such schools form part of the programme. They are then supported intensively during their first three weeks at high school, and then to a lesser degree during the remainder of the first term.

(2) *'High School' Pupils* — The programme of work for high school pupils is ten weeks, with the pupils spending half their time at the Attendance Centre following a PSE curriculum and the remaining time at the mainstream high school following the mainstream curriculum.

The Outreach Support Services

The provision of the Outreach Support Services is coordinated to link with the mainstream school provision by Individual Action Plans agreed with the school, parents and any other support agencies at Action Planning

Meetings. The plans are reviewed at least six-monthly if not sooner, and targets are set to guide the nature of the provision.

Issues of Reintegration

Dale Grove School and the Bankside Tutorial Unit operate a reintegration programme which involves all pupils and is an integrated part of the special provision so that possibilities of reintegration are always kept to the forefront of decision-making. The reintegration programme operates in three phases:

Phase One — This involves a termly identification of pupils who are considered ready for possible reintegration. These pupils are then placed on a six-week focused assessment which is monitored on a daily basis by all staff. At the end of the assessment period, staff review the progress of the identified pupils and decide: (a) whether a return to mainstream education is considered possible at this stage; or (b) whether a further period of assessment is necessary.

Phase Two — This involves a ten-week focused assessment in a mainstream school. Support is offered to the mainstream school and a guarantee that the place at Dale Grove or Bankside will remain open for the period of the placement.

Phase Three — A formal review of the Phase Two Assessment is held at the mainstream school with the headteachers in attendance, the assistant education officer, parents, the educational psychologist, the education welfare officer and the pupil. It is decided: (a) whether a full-time placement at the mainstream school should continue (involving an amendment to the statement); (b) whether there is need for an extended period of assessment at the mainstream school; or (c) a return to Dale Grove or Bankside is advisable at this point in time.

The emphasis of the Attendance Support Centre is on full-time reintegration into a mainstream high school within a fixed period of time. The Centre has succeeded in reintegrating pupils into all sixteen Tameside high schools. This success is achieved by developing close liaison between the pupil, parents, school teaching staff, education welfare staff, and the Centre staff. A common sense of purpose is developed and a common bond to want to achieve success.

The Hyde Unit, because of the timescale involved with year 11 pupils, is not usually concerned with reintegration.

In the present climate of examination result league tables and schools trying to improve their image, the reintegration of pupils with a background in special education, and particularly with emotional and behavioural difficulties, is a very contentious issue. In the past few years the service has had some success in reintegrating pupils, however, recently it has become more difficult to find schools, especially in the secondary phase, who are willing to give the pupil with emotional and behavioural difficulties a chance. There is the need to convince headteachers across all phases that it is not only in the best interest of the pupils to allow them access to mainstream education, but it also releases specialist provision both in terms of staff and facilities to support other pupils in need.

Developing the Strategy Further

The changing educational legislation makes it increasingly important to have clear policy statements, clear definitions of pupils' entitlement and service accountability, a clear operational model to guide service delivery, and clear policy-into-practice guidelines. These then need to be supported by clear strategies for matching provision to identified needs in a systematic and equitable fashion.

In line with the requirement for greater specificity within the overall process, the LEA is currently aiming to clarify three key components in matching provision to need:

- the profiling of needs in various 'Competency Areas';
- the profiling of special provision requirements;
- the criteria and 'trigger points' to be used in determining the levels of special provision to be made available within the service delivery model.

Such a clarification then needs to be supported with greater standardization in the strategy adopted in planning, implementing, monitoring and evaluating provision. It also needs to be supported with more explicit working arrangements; a specifying of rights and responsibilities; the evaluating of current 'service agreements' to ensure that they continue to be pertinent to need; and the reviewing of the Individual Action Planning procedures to ensure that they are given appropriate status in the overall educational system.

Reference

DFE (1994) *The Code of Practice for the Identification and Assessment of Special Educational Needs*, London, DFE Publications Centre.

Notes on Contributors

Peter Farrell is Course Tutor to the MSc Course in Educational Psychology, University of Manchester.

John Banks is an Educational Psychologist with Lancashire LEA.

Nick Boreham is Professor of Education in the Research and Graduate School, University of Manchester.

Pauline Collier is an Educational Psychologist and part-time Tutor in the Faculty of Education, University of Manchester.

John Cousil is Headteacher of the Tameside EBD Service.

Denise Craven is an Educational Psychologist with Birmingham LEA.

Roger Grimshaw is a senior Research Officer with the National Children's Bureau.

Georgina Hart is a Behavioural Support Teacher with Tameside LEA.

Kenneth McIntyre is an Educational Psychologist.

Vanessa Parffrey is a Lecturer in Education, University of Exeter and a Chartered Educational Psychologist.

Eric Peagam is a former special School headteacher and now works as an Educational Consultant for Cranmere Consultancies.

Ian Peers is a Lecturer in Education, University of Manchester.

Gareth Price is an Head of SEN Services, Tameside LEA.

Anne Rushton is an Associate Tutor, MSc in Educational Psychology University of Manchester and a senior Educational Psychologist with Manchester LEA.

Andy Samson is an Educational Psychologist with Tameside LEA.